With A Southern Exposure

With A Southern Exposure

BY

Furman Bisher

INTRODUCTION BY BING CROSBY

THOMAS NELSON & SONS

Edinburgh   NEW YORK   *Toronto*

TO

Montyne, Nicky, Roger, Jamie and Monte,
who live in it, and Southern Federal Savings & Loan,
which holds the mortgage.

Contents

Introduction

I imagine a great many people feel sure that the life of a sports writer is all beer and skittles, cakes and ale; preferred seats on the 50-yard line, back of home plate, at ringside, or where he can get a good view of Arnold Palmer lining up a 30-foot putt to win the Masters.

They see the sports writer mingling intimately with the great and near-great, the colorful old-timers and the zealous youngsters coming up, and when the afternoon or the evening is over, they feel all he has to do is file his story, amble to the local pub for the jolly times and the merry moments with other members of the craft.

Yes, a sports writer, if he's well connected, does have a broad entree. He gets around. He's with the action. But if he's going to rise in his field, he has to do a lot more than report the facts and figures, the state of the weather, the players' health, and the margin of victory.

The good ones, the outstanding writers, are those who can see the color, the personalities, and their relationships, the amusing and interesting sidelights, and can tell about them in the good earthy prose the sports follower understands and appreciates. I mean fellows like Rice, Lardner, Runyon, Kieran, to name but a few. Furman Bisher certainly qualifies. He has the touch. I particularly like his golf stories, being as I'm sort of a golf nut. In fact, I'd say Furman is really the O. B. Keeler of his day, and to Southern readers that's high praise indeed.

But this book of Furman's is really a mixed bag—stories about every sport and in every vein—knowledgeable, well-written yarns every reader will enjoy.

I congratulate the publishers for putting this material between covers.

BING CROSBY

Some in Their Glory

SHINOLA'S DAY TO SHINE

(Selected for "Best Sports Stories of the Year.")

(October, 1957)

(*Some athletes play an entire career with never a moment rich in glory. A fellow such as this was Vernal Jones, victim of the canine nickname of "Nippy."*

Jones had played several seasons with the St. Louis Cardinals, always managing to remain just another Jones boy. Then he was returned to the minor leagues, and after an operation on his back, was presumed to be of no further use for major league purposes.

Now, in the fourth game of the World Series, a retread from Sacramento thrown into a critical situation by the Milwaukee Braves as they played the New York Yankees, Jones finally collected his moment of glory. It was ironically fitting, for it was a drab, negative little moment— a man hit by a pitched ball. But it developed into a moment of drama on which was keyed the final outcome of the game.

I had started early for the clubhouse when Elston Howard hit his big home run. Trapped below in the stands, unable to return to the press box, I watched the concluding stage of the game from a box vacated by customers who left to beat the crowd, and I got a view of the "shoeshine pitch" that no one in the press box could see.

This was the last of "Nippy" Jones in the major leagues. He was returned to the minors that winter and soon drifted out of baseball.)

★ ★

MILWAUKEE—The little things in life can mean so very much, Mr. Vernal Jones, an amateur pundit and a most obscure Milwaukee Brave, pointed out Sunday afternoon.

Now you take the matter of keeping your shoes shined, or getting hit by pitched baseballs. Little things, of course, but in the course of his brief appearance at Milwaukee County Stadium on the Sunday matinee program, this Mr. Jones of Lynwood, California, playfully referred to as "Nippy," was able to demonstrate how such chaff as that can win a World Series game for you.

This was the day for Shinola to shine. As far as a fellow can find out, no shoe polish ever did this for a baseball team before. No such inconsequential item as a hit batsman ever won a game as important as the fourth game of the 1957 World Series between the Braves and the New York Yankees.

It is not polite to make light of the well-groomed Jones boy's flicker of activity in the game, a big, hectic number that was frightfully important in the recent affairs of the Braves. They had, to the satisfaction of several of the 45,804 clients who scurried to their cars with two Yankees out in the ninth, tied the World Series at two games each.

The Braves, worshipped locally with the blind, selfish devotion of small children, were leading the Yankees, 4–1. The way Warren Spahn was pitching there appeared to be justification for being first in your car in the parking lot. Since the first inning the Yankees had bruised the old left-hander for only four hits.

There were two men out and Yogi Berra, a spoiler, singled. The grand exodus continued. Gil McDougald singled. The exodus came to a grudging halt. Manager Fred Haney went out for a tete-a-tete with Spahn.

It must be household knowledge by this time that Haney had barely turned the knob on the water fountain back in the dugout when Spahn threw Elston Howard that pitch that Howard hit over the fence, and the score was tied, 4–4.

The way Spahn explained it later, he'd tried to keep the pitch low and outside. It turned out to be delinquent, low and inside, which is the way the dark brown Howard likes his serves.

The exodus turned now into a new charge back to the stands. People who had reached their cars and got the panicking news by radio rushed back to their seats. And then, for the first time in this previously uninspiring series, they saw baseball that moved the spirit and caused faint hearts to flutter.

In the tenth, the Yankees got another run. This was chiefly because Tony Kubek, a willful and resourceful traitor who was born here and went to New York to make a living, could outrun a slow bounder to Red Schoendienst, this also with two men out.

This was another triumph for the strategical genius, Charles D. Stengel, for he had only installed Kubek in the leadoff position this noon.

Hank Bauer tripled Kubek home and you could see Spahn fall limp on the mound. The old gentleman, who is immortal among National League pitchers, had given his best. He looked like a sure loser, for the Braves had had their hearts cut out, and nothing appeared surer now than death, taxes and defeat in five games.

This is where the obscure Mr. Jones, a handyman who conservatively hit .266 this season, appeared, his baseball shoes black and shiny. He is a journeyman imported from Sacramento because Joe Adcock broke a leg. He is not altogether new to this, for he was a pinch-hitter for the Cardinals in the 1946 World Series, and was once their regular first baseman.

Tommy Byrne threw a low pitch to Jones, who was invited to pinch-hit for Spahn in the tenth. The ball hit something and kept going. Jones leaped to Augie Donatelli's throat and contended that what it had hit was his right foot. Mr. Donatelli, an umpire, was equally as quick and argued otherwise.

While they carried on intensely, the ball, which had struck the grandstand wall and rebounded, rolled slowly between the two, its energy spent. Jones looked down, saw a black spot on the ball, picked it up and showed it triumphantly to Donatelli.

"The polish off my shoe!" he shrieked.

Umpire Donatelli gave in, Jones was sent to first base and there he was instantly succeeded as a base runner by Felix Mantilla, who also keeps his shoes shined.

It happened so fast that Casey Stengel had no chance to complain, and he still refused to after he had lost, an event that came about in manner so dramatic that all Wisconsin went home to work on a big hangover Sunday night.

Bob Grim was asked to relieve Byrne. Schoendienst, following proper procedure in such cases when you're a run behind and it's the witching hour, sacrificed Mantilla to second. Johnny Logan doubled and Mantilla scored.

This tied the game at 5–5. Then Ed Mathews hit a tall home run into the gap between the fence and the bleacher seats in right-field.

Now I suppose Mathews really ought to be the hero of this thing. There is nothing less heroic than a hit batsman and nothing more manfully expressive than a home run, but it wouldn't have happened if Jones hadn't reached base.

There is an appealing strain of simplicity woven into the fabric. It, for one thing, brings rare glory to one of the little things in baseball, such as department of non-distinction entitled "hit-by-pitcher," and also there is a moral to the story.

The moral is sartorial: Always keep your shoes shined.

WALTER NOBODY

(March, 1956)

(*This one is selected because it pictures Walter Alston at a time when it was obvious that he was out of place in the major leagues. He was so painfully human in contrast to the see-all, know-all, oratorical type generally envisioned as The Major League Manager that it seemed utterly ridiculous he should be managing the then Brooklyn Dodgers.*

The Dodgers had won the World Series from the New York Yankees, making Alston the supreme manager in baseball. This was strictly a stroke of luck, of course, he would be back on the farm at Montreal, or in Darrtown, Ohio, before long.

But, the longer he stayed the more solid he became. He survived transfer of the franchise to Los Angeles, a return of Charlie Dressen as coach, and of Leo Durocher as coach, and in time became dean of major league managers. This is a story of triumph for the simple, uncomplicated man, simple in this case as against complex.)

LAKELAND, FLA.—Walter Alston was sprawled out in the football stands adjacent to Henley Field like an alligator in the sun. His eyelids drooped lazily. He moved at half speed when he moved, usually to shoo away an inquisitive fly, or to scratch himself just to be scratching. When he smiled, the smile crept across his face slowly, like a tomcat having a pleasant dream.

The Brooklyn Dodgers had left the luxuries of Miami momentarily for an exhibition game with Detroit in the busy citrus belt. Over on Henley Field the Tigers were still having their batting practice. The Dodgers were waiting their turn to go on.

Two medium-sized boys wandered up, attracted by the bright blue trim of the foreign uniform.

"Do you play baseball?" one of them asked Alston.

"No, I'm just early for the football season," the Brooklyn manager said.

"Aw, he's a coach," said the boy's companion. "Can't you tell by his hair?"

"Lots of ball players are bald-headed. What's your batting average?" asked the first boy, turning to Alston again.

"I'm hitting .364," Alston said skillfully ignoring his lifetime major league average of .000 (0 for 1). "I expect to stick to that pace the rest of the year."

Another small boy came up with his father and asked for an autograph. The brash first youngster peered around Alston's elbow as he signed his name, then charged triumphantly back to his crony. "See," he said proudly, "I told you he didn't play. That's just the manager, Walter somebody."

For one full National League season, Alston was almost Walter Nobody. There was considerable doubt, especially among his own athletes, that Brooklyn had appointed a major league manager when he was promoted from the Montreal farm. Today, though he is manager of the world's champions of baseball, he is still relatively a Walter Nobody. Not Alston, but the class of the Dodgers is credited with the pennant and the World Series knockout.

There is much about Alston that substantiates this undercurrent of opinion. He is a plain man, painfully plain. He is not a dandy with repartee. He does not charm a dugout full of guests with rousing stories, complete with gestures. On the field, he might be taken for a farmer who came to manage the town team on a Saturday.

His relations with the press are morbidly routine. This does not inflate his rating with metropolitan authors, some of whom consider an Alston press conference the first cousin to a wake. He accepts and answers questions without embellishment.

"Are the Dodgers planning to sue Ted Williams for influ-

encing Johnny Podres' draft board into action?" a wise guy
asked.

A stoical Alston said, "We'd counted him out for the year,
anyway."

"What's your left-field picture like?"

"I can give you a lot of names," Alston said.

There was silence. "You want a list of names?" he asked.

"Sure, let's have a list of names."

He rattled off Sandy Amoros, Junior Gilliam, Dick Williams,
Jackie Robinson, Gino Cimoli, Bobby Wilson, Bert Hamric and
the ever popular George Shuba, Brooklyn's living memorial to
the wallflower.

"What's Robinson's status now? Does he have a position, or
would you classify him as a utility man?"

"He'll play where he'll do the most good," Alston said.

"How about Don Zimmer? What is he now?"

"The shortstop," Alston said. "Pee Wee Reese has been out
with a bad back."

"Does Ed Roebuck have to come back to make your bullpen
solid?"

"It wouldn't hurt any," Alston said. "We've got Clem Labine.
Don Bessent hasn't worked at all. He's been hurting. Jim
Hughes has looked better. He had a bad arm last year. Roebuck
just sort of lost his sinker."

"Have any rookies looked particularly good?"

"Chico Fernandez, Charlie Neal, Gino Cimoli and Dick Williams," he said. No embellishment, just answers.

Further investigation shows that of deepest concern to the
Dodgers right now is left-handed pitching. There has been an
acute shortage of left-handers in the left-handed borough of
Brooklyn since Preacher Roe retired. And now Podres is gone.

Everything else about the Dodgers remains, in the character of
Alston, solidly routine, Gil Hodges in his ninth season at first,
Reese in his fourteenth season at shortstop, Duke Snider in his
tenth season in right field, Roy Campanella in his ninth season
as catcher, and Gladys Gooding again at the console of the
mighty organ at Ebbets Field.

A FOUR-LEGGED FRAUD

(May, 1958)

(Attendance at the 1958 Kentucky Derby was marked by a decided tendency to ignore the sincere colts and spend time attending the court of a fraud from California named Silky Sullivan. Silky Sullivan had been winning races in the West by lagging far behind, then running over untalented opponents at the finish.

His finishes, the rich, red color of his hide, the bushy tail that trailed him like a witch's broom, and the general atmosphere of movieland phonyism that prevailed about him brought the curious to his stable in swarms. This was all over after the Derby was run. Silky ran only briefly. The next day he became a horse again and has spent considerable time since in obscurity.)

★ ★

LOUISVILLE—Silky Sullivan had left a call for 10 A.M. While this might be in keeping with his living habits as a West Coast parishioner, it is also significant that this unusual creature is the only Kentucky Derby horse on the grounds with a screened patio and music by Muzak.

Let alone that, he is also the leading attraction for all tourists who can politick a pass into the barn area at Churchill Downs. While this is no simple process itself, Silky Sullivan is drawing considerably more people than flies, for the common household insect can crash an exterminators' convention easier than he can get past this steed's austere line of civilian defense.

His stall is as distinctive as his personality. This screened facade has been constructed in front of his quarters, the lower half of the board painted redder than a Communist's conscience.

His stable boys wear red windbreakers, and at approximately 9:30 each morning a chunky fellow with a heavily bejowled face walks in and takes charge. He wore on this day a heavy lumberjack's coat, bright red with a broad stripe around the tail.

This was Reggie Cornell, Silky's trainer, and he did not seem to mind at all the turmoil in the area. When he opened the door to Silky's stall, photographers converged on him like a tidal wave.

"Will it bother him," asked a newsreel man, "if I bounce a light off the ceiling so he'll show up a little better?"

"Naw," said Cornell. "Nothing bothers him. Help yourself."

From somewhere appeared a pretty girl with sugar in her hand, and she fed Silky while the cameras ground and clicked, and in the custom of the trade, several of the photographic clerks kept saying, "Just one more, please."

"It's a good thing," said one amused observer, "that this is a horse of pleasant disposition, or he'd have that girl's right arm nibbled off up to the shoulder by now."

When they prepared Silky for his morning gallop, there was a tumultuous commotion in the area. Padded gear, also the startling shade of red, was broken out, and by the time Silky was ready for action he looked like a B-team tackle ready for dummy scrimmage.

Silky moved toward the track under an exercise boy named Pete Kozar and the area emptied completely. This is a rather late hour for a workout for a star of the track, and somebody suggested that Silky might be working on Pacific Standard Time.

"If he's running on Pacific Time Saturday," said a small clocker, "he'll be a little later getting in than the rest."

The background of Silky Sullivan is without the traditional thoroughbred distinction expected of a horse of some social standing in Kentucky. He was born by the mating of a stud named Sullivan and a mare named Lady N. Silk on the farm of a Dr. Riley H. Roberts in California.

His sire had produced a stakes winner named Sully's Trail in the Golden West, but had no racing history of his own to pass on to his offspring, nor did his dam. Cornell, who handles a stable of horses jointly owned by Philip Klipstein and Thomas Ross, joined these two California businessmen at the Delmar yearling sales two years ago and together they picked out Silky and bought him for a price of $10,700.

Physically, Silky is cut out in the pattern of Man O' War, a comparison that might be greeted with some gnashing of teeth around here. He is a huge animal, as was "Big Red," so thick at the withers that he appears to have some quarter-horse blood in his background. His coat is a sheeny red, and he stands out on a track like a blonde waiting for a street car. No larger colt has ever made this trip to Louisville, and with his vivid characteristics, he is a beauteous thing to behold.

Out on the track, Silky was a most cooperative fellow. He snorted and puffed like an old railroad engine, and bowed his head, indicating fury, as he came within camera range.

"That's the way he is all the time," Cornell said with obvious pride. "He's never been no trouble a-tall. He's trained ever which way I could ask him."

"When he first showed this tendency to lag back," a man asked Cornell, "did you try to break him of it?"

"Well," said Cornell, "he didn't do it until he raced the first time, and then he come on and won it breezing. You don't want to change Mickey Mantle's stance if he's hitting home runs, so I let him run this way."

"And so you didn't try to do anything about it, Reggie?"

"Naw," he said. "There's nothing wrong with him, except he don't like to get hit in the face with clods of dirt."

When the congregation returned to the barn, a quiet-natured roan was being hot-walked under the shed, but everybody was too busy with the celebrity to pay any attention. It would have made no difference whatsoever had they known this tired but honest beast was Gone Fishin' twice straight a winner over the celebrated Mr. Sullivan. After all, all this colt can do is run.

MURTAUGH THE PERSISTENT

(December, 1960)

(Major league manager of the year in 1960, A.D., was a dumpy, chisel-chinned Irishman from Chester, Pennsylvania, named Daniel Edward Murtaugh. He had reached the major leagues because he was, if not a failure, surely no conspicuous success in the minor leagues.

Out of work as a manager, he had been hired as a coach by the Pittsburgh Pirates. When Bobby Bragan was fired as manager in 1957, Murtaugh got the job only because he happened to be handy, and for the interim only, of course.

One of baseball's longest interims achieved a startling climax when Pittsburgh won the National League pennant and coarsely ignored logic by winning the World Series from the New York Yankees in 1960.

Here, now, was Murtaugh, being glad-handed from pillar to post at the winter baseball meeting in Louisville, Kentucky, the same dumpy, chisel-chinned, disparaged manager of the minor leagues four seasons before, bit-marked distinctively now by the stripe of success.)

★ ★

LOUISVILLE—Danny Murtaugh had just walked in out of the frigid afternoon. A cold and gusty wind had blown in from the north and Louisville shivered in its boots. Murtaugh stood just inside the door for a moment, rubbing his chilled hands together, making a noise like a snorting horse, surveying the lobby of the Kentucky Hotel, milling with baseball people, and this is when the notion struck me.

Here was a guy who is representative of all the persistence

in baseball. You hear a fellow out of work saying he's determined to stay in the game. On occasion you'll feel sorry for one who says it, for you know he ought to be doing something else and getting on with his life.

But many are like Danny Murtaugh. They know nothing else but baseball. Danny knows how to sell men's clothing. The winning of the world's championship at Pittsburgh failed to make a celebrity out of him.

When the World Series was done, Danny went home to Chester, Pennsylvania, and resumed his old winter job of clerking in a men's store.

Murtaugh became a major league manager by accident. The man who has stood behind him, Joe Brown, the Pirates' general manager, also stood behind him as they scanned the hotel lobby.

Joe was Murtaugh's commandant at New Orleans, where Danny managed for three or four years without outstanding success. One season a team he had in first place at All-Star time managed to finish out of the first division. The cruel fans of New Orleans ate him alive from the grandstand, and this was in the time when baseball fans were still coming out to see the Pelicans play.

"In most towns they'll call you a bum if they don't like you," Ellis Clary said. "In New Orleans, they went a little further on Murtaugh. They called him a tramp, with a few other adjectives thrown in."

In Atlanta, I remember one leather-lunged box seat-holder who made a habit of tormenting poor Danny. "Hey, Murtaugh!" he'd holler, "Where do you get your plastic surgery done?"

Danny never was the handsomest fellow in the world, with that Irish jaw and Roman nose.

Murtaugh was in truth fired at New Orleans, a sort of mercy release. He was later fired at Charleston, West Virginia, but he came up with something when Joe Brown got to Pittsburgh and Bobby Bragan became manager of the Pirates. He became a coach.

When Bragan was fired, Murtaugh was appointed to fill in. Apparently that was all it was, an interim appointment.

But here it is three years later and Murtaugh is not only still on the job, but also the conqueror of the world. There has never been a more humble conqueror, and to all of these fellows who swear a devotion to the game of baseball, he stands as a symbol.

Here is a man who gives them a reason not to give up. No matter how hammered-down you may get, stay with it. Out of a pile of ashes may arise a garden of roses.

All of this was running through my mind because Clary, the Valdosta (Ga.) pool room magnate, was standing with me. He is attending the fifty-ninth minor league baseball convention as a member of the vast unemployed. He was fired off the coaching staff of the late Washington Senators last month.

"Some people say that they resigned," Clary said. "I didn't resign. I was fired. Kicked out. When Cookie Lavagetto got the authority, he fired me as quick as he could."

Clary said, "I want to stay in baseball, but I don't want any part of the minor leagues. I either want to coach in the majors, or get a scouting job and stay home in Valdosta and rack them balls when I'm not on the road. I'm getting to be a pretty good rack boy.

"This managing in the minors is only good for one thing—to get you fired. You stay a year and move on. I don't like that."

He would concede, he said, that everything was not heavenly in the majors, and he had a story to illustrate.

"Bill Wight, the left-handed pitcher, had driven with his family all the way from California to Florida for spring training one year. He's just getting into St. Petersburg when he hears on the car radio that he has been traded by the Yankees to the White Sox, who are training three miles from his home in California.

"I laugh every time I think of this story," Clary explained, "because the fellow that wrote it said that a policeman in St. Pete gave Wight special permission to make a U-turn on Water Street and head back to California."

Everybody has tried to analyze the sudden overwhelming success of Murtaugh, this former classic failure. No one has done it satisfactorily, including Murtaugh.

It seems that he decided not to try to manage too much, but to give his athletes their rein and let them go. Then, gaining full momentum, he was swept up by the spiritual tide and carried away with it, careful at all times not to press the genius button.

"That's me," Clary said, "never overwork that genius button."

About this time a silver-haired old gentleman walked past and he and Clary howdy-ed.

"There was a great manager who never got anywhere," Clary said, "Tommy Thomas, the old pitcher. He managed at Baltimore when I played there, and he was one of the best."

"Was he there when you went into stands after a fan?" Sid Hartman of Minneapolis asked.

"Was he there?" Clary echoed. "He sent me in the stands after the guy, the mealy-mouth blankety-blank so-and-so.

"Right after that, by the way, I got one of the funniest telegrams I ever saw in my life. Old Morris Frank, my friend in Houston, the newspaperman, read about it in the paper and he sent me a wire that read like this:

" 'Stay out of the stands, my friend. At your age, you'll get there soon enough.' "

THE REFORMATION OF JOEY JAY

(October, 1961)

(Joey Jay is remembered by most of us as the silently angry type young man. He'd never had much to say before, and when he said it, it sounded as if it came from an apprentice Jack Hurley. It seemed he suffered from chronic dyspepsia. He held an endurance record for the pout.

Manhood had been thrust upon him when Milwaukee traded him to Cincinnati. It was like the severance of the silver cord. He had grown up in the lap of the Braves and had been petted and coddled.

Shaken by this uprooting, he had accepted his burden of adulthood and won twenty-one games for the Reds, followed by victory in the World Series. Suddenly he felt his team revolving about him, conqueror of the mighty Yankees, and he responded with the maturity of a leader.

It was a rewarding moment to stand there and watch him conduct himself in so genteel a manner. A 24-year-old baby had grown up at the age of 25.)

NEW YORK—The reformation of Joey Jay is complete. He was a bad boy. Not bad in the terms of vice, dope addiction, boozing, kleptomania, that sort of thing. Simply bad in the terms of obstinance, sulkiness, social rebellion, that sort of thing.

He had subdued the New York Yankees by a score of 6–2 on four hits. His huge frame, six feet, four inches high and 215 pounds large, was totally surrounded in the Cincinnati dressing room by screaming photographers and inquisitive journalists. Through it all, he maintained composure and was gracious.

On Wednesday evening, he and the mother of his four children had gone to see "The Unsinkable Molly Brown." He had been unable to sit restfully through it. He was worrying about being worried about pitching against the Yankees in the second game of the World Series.

His dad walked up to the fringe of the crowd in the club-house. Over their heads, clamoring, shouting questions, pressing him and all, he caught a glimpse of his sire. Amid the turmoil and the flashing of flash bulbs, he said: "Hi, Pop. Thanks for everything."

This was a thank you to the whole world for putting up with Joey Jay during his stage of petulance. In Atlanta, for instance, they'd had to hustle him out of town after a Sunday-afternoon obscenity directed toward a colony of jeering fans.

This was in 1956. There were more unproductive seasons to follow. He won seven, he won six and he won nine for Milwaukee, far below the production potential in that ripe right limb of his.

"I was sort of by myself," he said. "I felt the resentment that the other players felt for me because I had come in with more bonus money than a lot of them had made. I stayed to myself. Now I know how they felt."

He was downright surly in those days. Conversation came painfully with him. When he had to miss his starting turn in the 1958 World Series, when Milwaukee played the Yankees, Fred Haney, his manager, inferred that he was unrighteously abandoning a vowed responsibility.

Now he held up a hand in the Cincinnati dressing room, his left hand. "The finger was broken," he said. "The doctor told me not to play because I might suffer permanent injury."

Now he had won twenty-one games for Cincinnati, and now he had beaten the Yankees in the World Series. All of a sudden, the clouds cleared away. He spoke as a man who had several things on his mind that he wanted to unload.

"All of the abuse I took in those first years in Milwaukee I earned," he said. "I felt my own teammates resented me. I resented them for resenting me. I probably never would have won in Milwaukee. I had to get out of there.

"I won this year because I got a chance to pitch on a regular schedule. Fred Hutchinson has been a good manager to me. He has come out to the mound and coaxed me. He has come out and chewed me out real good. But he's got great timing. Every time he did what he did, it seemed to be what I needed.

"This has been a great year. This is a great game to win. But I don't put it above the game in Chicago, when we won and Los Angeles lost and we won the pennant. I had been on a pennant winner before, but I was so much a part of this one.

"And when I won my twentieth game, and this one. These are my big ones."

There was a strange sort of seriousness on his face as he said these things. He drove home points that he must have wanted to drive home for many months. In Joey Jay's own mind, he could now answer up to the world that had come to regard him as a spoiled brat.

The game Jay pitched against the Yankees was as masterful in its own way as the game Whitey Ford had pitched the day before. Ford had had to brook no resistance. Jay had.

Jay had fought his way out of it with some splendid craftsmanship. He toyed with Roger Maris, who now is in danger of becoming the least illustrious player of the series.

He threw only one really damaging pitch, which Yogi Berra returned to the right-field stands.

Jay's own heavy artillery had been silenced for a second day. In the big rallies, Vada Pinson and Frank Robinson had been rendered null and void. Instead, the young and the unlicensed people had rushed to his side with offense.

Gordon Coleman, the square-jawed first baseman, had struck the introductory blow, a two-run home run that gave him a lead. Then Elio Chacon, the little Venezuelan, had made off with home plate right out from under Elston Howard's nose, and this was the eventual winning run.

Actually, it was no more Howard's fault than Ralph Terry's.

Howard pursued the escaped pitch with his eye on Eddie Kasko, fearing Kasko might dash for second. Terry failed to cover the plate, and no one, least of all Howard, expected the daring Chacon to make a break for it.

Then John Edwards, the boy catcher who batted .182 and drove in nine runs this season, responded to insult with two blows that drove in two runs. The Yankees had chosen to walk Gene Freese twice to pitch to Edwards, a student at Ohio State University, and Edwards had singled and doubled, and you could hear the crashing of strategical china in the Yankee kitchen.

Now it is even. They move to Cincinnati's obtuse little nook. The fences are close. Cincinnati's pitchers are accustomed to this hazard. Yankee pitchers are not. A rabbit in his own briar patch is much harder to catch than in foreign briar patches.

SIC TRANSIT GLORIA
(December, 1960)

*(This was somewhat off my beat. Ice hockey and I are faintly
acquainted, but I happened in on a stirring evening at Madison Square
Garden on this visit to New York.*

*The sight of this lump of a man in his heroic moments of goal-tending
was soon offset by the pathetic sight of him suffering the scorn of the
galleryites who only moments before had been standing to cheer him.*

*This is the law of the jungle, though. Hail the mighty and those that
prevail, damn the weak and the fallen. Gump Worsley accepted his fate
as such, and his glory, as he felt it, was only temporarily snatched away
from him.)*

★ ★

NEW YORK—Precisely at the hour that the opening face-
off had been scheduled at Madison Square Garden Sunday evening, some 9,000 hearties who had mushed through the early
stages of a blizzard to watch the New York Rangers play the
Boston Bruins listened rather cynically to this apologetic announcement:

"Ladies and gentlemen, due to the poor travel conditions, several of the Rangers are late arriving for the game. The start will
be delayed for a short while. We beg your kind indulgence."

Somehow, I couldn't imagine the Yankees delaying the start
of a baseball game because Mickey Mantle and Whitey Ford
were late arriving from the Copacabana. And besides, this was
an ice hockey player's kind of weather. They could have skated

in from Long Beach, a settlement out on Long Island where many of the Rangers are colonized.

"American drivers!" Lorne (Gump) Worsley snorted in the Rangers dressing room. "They don't know how to drive in this stuff. We got stuck in a jam trying to get to the subway station because the clucks can't drive in snow. It wasn't our fault."

Gump Worsley tends goal for the Rangers. He is five feet, six inches tall and built on the order of an Idaho potato.

"I'm five pounds overweight," he said out of the side of his mouth, as if confiding in a new admirer.

He reached into his pocket, pulled out a dental bridge and fitted it in his mouth, closing up a gap between his front teeth. Thus restored to his original beauty, he muttered a verbal pungency or two, as if to remind himself that he had no right to appear gay.

Ol' Gump is sort of the Bobo Newsom or Boots Poffenberger of ice hockey. More Newsom than Poffenberger because Bobo was a big performer and so is Gump.

On the evening before in Boston, Gump had shut out the Bruins. On this evening in New York, he had them shut out again and he had a stretch of 167 scoreless minutes working when hell froze over.

The Rangers were leading, 2–0, on goals scored by Harry Howell and Johnny Wilson in the first period. Gump was having a magnificent evening. I had been in New York only a short time, but already I had a new hero, as un-heroic a looking figure as this fat little man presents.

Garmented for action and standing alone at his station in front of the nets, Gump Worsley looks somewhat like a tub of lard poured into a pair of old hip boots. This, naturally, increases one's affection for him, for he appears to be such a forlorn outcast.

All goalies in hockey give the impression that they live in a permanent state of ostracism, as they stand guarding the mouth of the nets, fight off furious attacks of the enemy, and then are left to their loneliness again.

It is said to be a trade involving great mental pressure. "Not for me it ain't," Gump said. "It may be for other guys, but not me."

This is the Bobo in him. He merely feels that Gump Worsley is the best damn goal-tender in ice hockey and he feels sorry for all the others. And that is that.

It was just a couple of years ago that Terry Sawchuck, who, with all due respect to Gump Worsley, was the giant among hockey goalies at that time, disappeared from the Boston Bruins. He was found sitting in a bar a few days later complaining about the mental hazards of goal-tending and how life had been so unfair with him.

Presently, Sawchuck is employed by the Detroit Red Wings. His stature has diminished considerably. He is now the second-string goalie in Detroit.

What happened to Gump Worsley Sunday evening shouldn't happen to a pickpocket. He was going on 167 minutes of shut-out goal-tending. The Rangers led, 2–0. The 9,000 mushers were happy. The game was almost over. Gump was being hailed from the galleries. Every save was cheered, for now he was threatening perfection.

When suddenly what should happen? The Bruins score two goals on him in forty-seven seconds and the game ends in a tie.

In a prolonged scuffle in front of Worsley's little netted office, John Bucyk, a Bruin forward from Edmonton, Alberta, slipped the puck past the lumpy little defender. Then in a similar situation a few moments later, Don McKenney, who comes from Smith Falls, Ontario, darted out of a wrangling pack of armored skaters and scored another. He may as well have stabbed Ol' Gump right through the gizzard.

Gump's knighthood was ended. The house came down on him now. As he skated off the ice at the end, some bitter patron in the upper balcony aimed a handful of garbage at him.

Gump, lonely, pathetic little butterball, turned and hurled a futile challenge at his attacker. He shook his fist and made a gesture inviting the jeering guest outside, but two teammates skated by and took their wounded little goalie with them to cool off in private quarters.

And so Ol' Gump cursed his ill fortune. Nine years he has been a Ranger, off and on, for he has had his ups and his downs. No more than a year ago he was farmed out to Kitchener, Ontario, when he allowed himself to bloat out of shape. But he was back shortly.

Nine years of this, 31 years old and great fame, feature stories in sports magazines, picture on the covers and all that, and it gets away from him at the last tantalizing moment.

It had, honestly, seemed as much the failure of the Rangers defense men, Bill Gadsby and Irv Spencer, as it was the failure of Worsley. In a dingy parlor outside the dressing room, Worsley's commandant, Murray Patrick, general manager of the Rangers, was defending him with the same type of logic.

"It was the defense men's fault," Patrick said. "They were squatting down like a goalie instead of standing straight up. I don't want my defense men playing goalie.

"Worsley's enough for me. He was having one helluva night."

Thus restored to immortality, Ol' Gump should have trundled off to Long Beach and had himself a good night's sleep.

Some on the Rise

DO YE KEN VENTURI?

(April, 1956)

(Ken Venturi was nobody at this time, but he was about to become somebody. This was in the early stage of the most tragically successful event in his life. Everything that he has done in golf since can be traced in some way to this flirtation with immortality in Augusta, Georgia.

He almost won the Masters in 1956, a brash, clear-eyed amateur player 24 years old, just out of the Army. He missed because on the fourth round he was so overwhelmed with the sudden realization of what he was about to achieve that he used 80 strokes to play the last 18 holes, and Jack Burke eased in ahead of him.

Whereupon Venturi became a boy again. He cried unashamed tears like a little boy. The big bully Burke had stolen his candy. It was cruel.

But here we find Venturi in a light-hearted moment, glorying in his lead, happy, unburdened by cares, oblivious to the bitter prospect that any manner of disaster might ever befall him.)

AUGUSTA, Ga.—It was a gusty Friday morning at Augusta National, very gusty. A playboy wind nipped devilishly at the fetlocks of the lovely chicks. And bolder gusts reached a little higher.

On the clubhouse driveway a woman dressed fit to kill was almost run down by a driver looking in the other direction at another doll dressed fit to kill.

Out on the clubhouse lawn, under a large umbrella, a mother

spoon-fed a baby. She was surely a golfer's wife, for she never missed a shot.

The wind had blown out a chunk of the big scoreboard that stands like a highway billboard between the tenth and eighteenth holes. Out on the course the fairways were like wind tunnels. Inside the clubhouse the door to the locker room on the second deck—"gentlemen only"—opened precisely at 12:16 and one of the youngest vice presidents in the country reported for work.

Ken Venturi carried a little satchel in one hand. He wore a tweedy coat and an expression that said absolutely nothing. It didn't say he was nervous, he was relaxed, he wished it was Sunday night, or wonder what the 'ell he was doing here? "here" meaning on top of the pile at the Masters.

"He looks like he's half asleep," somebody said.

"Maybe he's still dreaming," somebody else said.

Remember, this is a 24-year-old father of three weeks who teed off Thursday morning with a gallery that was following him because he happened to be paired with Billy Joe Patton. He is, by USGA standards, an amateur, for he doesn't take money for playing. He is, or was, relatively unrenowned, though he has been a member of the Walker Cup team. He has played little recently in tournaments of note, almost as if he had been holding his big game for this one.

But the point is, no more than two or three out of ten people could have told you Thursday morning who Ken Venturi is.

Venturi sat down at a long table and ordered some orange juice.

"Are you nervous?" an untactful beast asked him.

Venturi grinned a nice Italian grin. "Yeah," he said. "I'm such a wreck I couldn't sleep but ten and a half hours last night."

Ashford Smith grunted. He's an Atlantan and Harvie Ward's brother-in-law. The three of them are sharing quarters in one of the club's cottages. "Sleep?" Ashford hooted. "The maids cleaned up the room. Everybody else dressed and left and he kept sleeping.

"And the noises he makes. He doesn't snore." Ashford made some funny grunts and snorts and gurgles, sort of like a sick rhinoceros. "Like that. He'd scare you to death to sleep in the same room with him if you didn't know what it was."

All the time the locker room door to the porch was opening and closing and the wind howled in furiously. It was like a scene in an old movie about the Yukon. Freddie Haas, Ed Furgol, Tommy Bolt and Dick Chapman came in and fought the door shut. Then they huffed and puffed and blew on their hands like men coming in out of a snowstorm.

The wind whistled through a crack in a big window and made a fearful noise.

"I don't mind the wind," Venturi said, "especially if it's match play. What's happening to you is happening to the guy you're playing, so it's the same. It's tougher in medal play, but I don't mind it. I'll just have to keep my curve ball a little lower today."

"Were you here the year it hailed?" Henry Picard, one of the elder statesmen said. "It came right through my umbrella, hailstones big as mothballs. In Greensboro one year they had to hold up their tournament for two days on account of a snowstorm in late March. The fire department tried to wash the stuff off the streets, I remember, and the water froze as quick as it hit the pavement."

"Have you ever seen it this windy over here before?" Venturi asked.

"I've seen it windy," Picard said. "Maybe it was this windy, I don't know. I've seen it plenty windy."

"Well," Venturi said, "I don't mind the wind, anyway. I hope it don't blow up any rain out there."

There has been limited tournament experience for Venturi since he came out of the Army. He has had to become readjusted to his business in San Francisco. Through the courtesy of golfing devotee Ed Lowrey, who maintains a sort of an amateur golf stable in San Francisco, Venturi is the vice president of an automobile dealership.

Somebody said the other day it should be called Ed Lowrey's academy of golf, Byron Nelson, headmaster. For Nelson has spent a good deal of the time working with the Lowrey colts.

Venturi played last in the Phoenix Open and finished fifth. "Oh, I played in the city tournament," he said. "I played Ward in the finals. You know how many people were there? Ten thousand were in the gallery that day."

Venturi won. The next day Mrs. Venturi presented him his trophy, a small baby boy.

The door opened again and blew his napkin off the table for about the twelfth time. It seemed to remind him that the great out-of-doors was calling. "Well," he said, "I'd better go."

It seemed like a reasonably good place to end a column, and I went, too.

ARNOLD PALMER'S FIRST BIG ONE

(Selected for "Best Sports Stories of the Year.")

(April, 1958)

(Usually when a golfer begins the last round of a tournament in a tie for the lead, he postpones his hotel checkout until a decision has been reached. Tied with Sam Snead at this juncture of the 1958 Masters, Arnold Palmer was not figured to get the best of it, for he was not then the dominant figure in the game that he is today.

This became his first big victory. Snead fell back and Palmer beat off Ken Venturi with that big blow on the twelfth hole.

When it was over, one fellow asked, "How can you be sure it was positive thinking? Maybe Palmer was being negative about it, positive he wasn't going to be able to take Snead."

You'll always find one like this in almost every crowd.)

AUGUSTA, GA.—Precisely at the hour of 10:32 Easter Sunday morning, Arnold Palmer stepped up to the cashier's window at the Richmond Hotel and checked out, seven and one-half hours before he was to be suited out in a green sport jacket.

At the moment he was leg-locked in a tie with Sam Snead for the lead in the Masters golf tournament, a little festival near and dear to all golf players in this world.

"Isn't this a brash display of optimism?" a fellow asked Palmer.

"Positive thinking," said the golfer, winking with hearty good will, "just positive thinking."

Well, before the day was spent, and before Palmer scored his 73 and won the tournament, an abundance of positive thinking had been required. It happens that on this final round, Palmer is paired with Ken Venturi, who is hungering for a Masters championship like nobody else has ever hungered.

On the very first hole there is dramatic action. You see, actually not many people are thinking in terms of Palmer. He is a young fellow and he has won more tournaments in 1958 than any other professional. He won at Houston, at Wilmington, at Akron and at San Diego.

But he is still Arnold Palmer, and he is not a notable figure among the professionals. Besides, as a man who can remember him as an undergraduate at Wake Forest, when Jim Weaver was driving the car and signing the tabs for the golf team, you can only think of him in terms of a boy.

Venturi, who is three strokes behind Snead and Palmer, is charging the field, and he comes into the first hole with a recovery shot that leaves him thirty-five or forty feet from the cup. Venturi sinks his putt stylishly. Snead comes along a few minutes later and he takes an humbling six on the same hole, and so your arithmetic shows you that Venturi has picked up three strokes on one of the leaders on the first hole.

But nobody really is thinking of Palmer. They are thinking of Snead as the leader, and as the guy Venturi has got to beat.

Pretty soon Snead has blown it. It is like 1951, when he goes into the last round tied with Skee Riegel for the lead, and when he works feverishly over a cool 80, and Ben Hogan wins it.

"I never drove so well and scored as bad in my life," Snead said when he arrived in the clubhouse. He was in a good humor, and there was no bitterness. What he couldn't control was his long irons, and these golf players tell you that the most important shot on most any hole is the second shot, which is usually a long iron.

Well, the Venturi and Palmer twosome makes the turn and Venturi has picked up a stroke on Palmer. You can sense that the nice, young Californian is about to make his move. He is determined to win this thing.

I guess that if you get to a turning point, you begin at the twelfth hole. This is a par three, and this is where the controversy comes up, almost a baseball-style controversy in which the players and the umpires come to a crisis.

Palmer overshoots the green and the ball lands in a muddy bank, almost buried out of sight. There is a consultation. Rules committeemen come up and they have a look, and they look at one another, and say, "Well, what do you think of this?"

Finally, one of them turns to Venturi and says, "What do you think of this? Should Palmer have to play the imbedded ball, or drop one and play it?"

Venturi says, "Well, I think he ought to be allowed to drop one and play it, but I hope he has to play the imbedded ball."

He wants to win the tournament.

The rules committeemen, after a meeting at the summit, finally let Palmer play the imbedded ball, on which he scores a five, and then let him play a provisional ball on which he scores a three.

Nobody knows anything, especially five or six thousand people in the gallery. By the time Venturi and Palmer and their gallery reach the fifteenth fairway, they get the official decision. Palmer is allowed a three instead of a five on No. 12, and these are the strokes by which he wins the tournament.

Of course, since that time the stout Wake Forest alumnus has scored an eagle on No. 13, and these two strokes also win it for him.

Palmer goes on and he scores his 73 and finishes 284 and he looks pretty safe. But he is not safe yet until Doug Ford and Fred Hawkins, who are playing in a twosome, both have missed long putts on No. 18 when either one could have sunk it and tied.

Palmer is dressed out in his new green coat in the ceremony on the practice green and it is all over. There is a lot of history in the press tent, where Palmer tells about himself, because he is still mostly a stranger.

His daddy is the professional at a nine-hole course in Latrobe, Pennsylvania, and this is still his home. "When I get in trouble with my game," he said, "my daddy is still the one I run to. I go home and he works on my game. I've been nothing but a golf player since I was five years old, and I've been waiting for a day like this."

He won the National Amateur one year, and now he wins this. No other National Amateur champion has ever won the Masters before. I keep thinking of Ford, who had predicted that he would win, and Venturi who had thought he would win. But the most positive thinker of all was Arnold Palmer, who checked out of his hotel room Sunday morning, and he won.

A NATURAL-BORN HOME RUN HITTER

(March, 1957)

(*Dick Stuart had never played a game in the major leagues. Frankly, at this stage I never thought he ever would. He was an unpolished rookie full of brashness, over-confidence and a resentment for defense. He felt the major leagues needed him, a fellow who had hit sixty-six home runs in a season.*

As it turned out, Stuart was right about Stuart. He was turned out to the minor leagues once more, which he felt was a serious mistake of major-league judgment, but he was back in 1958. In 1960, Pittsburgh won a World Series with him playing first base, something that never even the wildest dreamer would ever have conceived. It was Stuart's opinion, though, that it would never have been possible without him.)

FORT MYERS, Fla.—There was a right-handed hitting outfielder named Dick Stuart who hit sixty-six home runs for Lincoln, Nebraska, last summer. This achievement seemed to catch the eye of the Pittsburgh Pirates, who invited the mighty slugger to spend spring training with them in this drowsy, tropical settlement devoted to the age of Edison.

It is entirely possible that Fort Myers has not seen the like of Dick Stuart since Edison made camp here. You can tell, in other words, that a genius is in town. If you don't believe it, just stand outside the left-field fence at Terry Park, or better yet, gather around the batting cage.

"That's him," said Bobby Bragan, who manages the Pirates.

"No. 5. He'll probably hit one out for you. He will hit one out if he knows you're watching him."

Stuart also drove home 158 runs and struck out 171 times at Lincoln, but this last statistic doesn't disturb the Pirates a great deal. For a fellow hitting sixty-six home runs, it doesn't make a lot of difference how he's going out if he's going out. What does bother the Pirates is that Stuart is no James J. Piersall, star of stage, screen and defense, in the field.

"It's up to his glove," Bragan said, "whether he stays or not. He's going to have to show me he can field. Up to now he has been frightened at the sight of a fungo stick."

It is a reluctant Stuart who marches somberly to the outfield with glove in hand. A few days ago, after a rather shabby exhibition, Bragan sentenced him to a postgame clinic on defense. Coach Sam Narron fungoed him from one side of left field to the other until Stuart finally lost his lunch. But never a whimper came out of him.

The Pirates survived—financially—their worst baseball depression on a similar type. Ralph Kiner drove the ball far but was no gem with the glove on. He filled the park, however, obviously with people whose defensive taste was bad, but whose cash was as green as spring.

"Stuart is a better fielder than Kiner," Jack Hernon, a Pittsburgh author, said. "At least he can throw."

With this encouragement, it seemed the proper time to approach the apprentice. "Will you excuse me a few minutes?" he said. "I promised this fellow I'd go on the radio at one-fifteen."

It might be said here that Stuart has been the journalistic redemption of a rather dull crop of rookies this spring in Florida. He did not, as you may have suspected, come out of a Ring Lardner book. He is no screwball. He is merely a greedy young giant who came to hit home runs and nothing else. There is nothing wrong with a lively single, but give him a good, healthy home run any time.

As true as his word, he was back in a few minutes and obliging. "I think I can hit this pitching," he said. "I hit three home runs the first three games, then I tapered off some. I've been to bat fifteen times and had four hits and struck out five times. The first time I stepped into the batting cage I hit four out of the park in ten swings."

"How does a fellow go about hitting sixty-six home runs in a season, Dick?"

"Sixty-eight," he corrected. "I hit two in the playoffs.

"I don't know. You tell me. There are some short fences in the Western League, but not that many. When I hit 'em, they stay hit."

There was a question of previous minor league experience.

"I've played three years," Stuart said. "I hit thirty-four home runs at Billings, Montana, then went into the Army. I hit fifty-five in service, but the pitching was lousy. I came back and started off at New Orleans, but they just used me for pinch-hitting. I'm not much of a pinch-hitter. I went back to Billings and hit thirty-one more home runs in about ninety-two games."

Stuart's production dwindled to a trickle near the close of the season at Lincoln.

"That's right," he said. "I got hit on the knuckle and it swelled up. Then I was pressing, trying to break the record of seventy-two. In the last thirty games I didn't hit but five home runs and I struck out fifty times."

"They say you have trouble with your fielding, Dick."

"My fielding isn't too good," he said, "but I've got a pretty good arm. If I have a fault, I guess that's it, fielding."

"Do you expect to stick with the Pirates this season?"

"If I don't, it's their mistake," he said.

Stuart is the 24-year-old son of a dry cleaning plant operator in Culver City, California. He holds a union card as a movie extra. Physically, his craft is trimmed along the lines of Ted Williams, bulky mid-riff and sloping shoulders, and for a pattern a kid could have worse. He lived miserably as a child, for he was a senior in high school before he hit his first home run. He was a catcher when a scout named Bob Fontaine signed him for Pittsburgh.

In due time the Pirates and the White Sox called the day's meeting to order, and Billy Pierce, a substantial left-hander, was at work for Chicago. Stuart approached with a bat in hand and a man on base, and he swung on the first pitch. When last seen it was disappearing over a sign that read 377 feet and I left the park as he trotted lazily around the bases.

He made it look so easy to play in the major leagues.

THE RUNT OF THE LITTER

(December, 1956)

(I drove up a country road into a farm yard where an old station wagon with "Lulubelle" painted on the side sat in dilapidated resignation. There was a pitcher's mound just off the front porch. Mitt Lary, the head of the Lary clan, said he had sat on this porch and taught his boys how to pitch.

Since I was on an assignment for Sport Magazine, *I couldn't use all of this rich material in a newspaper column. But there was still enough left to tell of the emergence of Frank Lary as a premium baseball pitcher.*

It looked as though he was on the way to an extended career of sensationalism. Unfortunately, it didn't work that way. It was five years later before he had another big season. In the meantime, though, he kept on beating the New York Yankees and learned how to play the electric guitar, which means he wasn't exactly standing still.)

★ ★

NORTHPORT, Ala.—There are seven sons of Mitt and Margaret Lary, Rte. 3, Northport, Alabama—Joe, James, Raymond, Ed, Al, Frank and Gene. Of the seven, Frank is the smallest but also the greatest.

This became so on September 23, the day that Frank Lary beat Cleveland on a two-hitter that was a no-hitter for seven and one-third innings. It became the twentieth victory of his season. A few days later he added No. 21, which made him the biggest winner of the American League season, and the first Detroit Tiger to win that many since Hal Newhouser in 1947.

This is not all that makes him great. What makes him greater is the way the twenty-one victories came off.

Normally, twenty-one game winners are invited to perform in the major league All-Star game. Frank, however, saw the game on television, and then took his wife, Emma Lou, out to loll around on the sands of Metropolitan Beach in Detroit.

This oversight was purely and simply Lary's. He had neglected to win more than four games by the time the All-Star voters went to the polls. Fact is, at that time he led the American League in defeats, with ten. He had been knocked out more times than an addle-brained prize fighter.

This evoked pure amazement in Detroit, where he had won fourteen and lost fifteen his rookie season. He had looked so smart in the spring that Bucky Harris started him on opening day, an honor usually reserved for veterans like Steve Gromek, Ned Garver or Virgil Trucks, not a sophomore.

Lary got beat on opening day, but for twenty-four hours he led the league in home runs. The only run Detroit scored in a 2–1 defeat by the Yankees was his own homer.

Things never squared off for him for the longest time. Frank did manage to beat the Yankees, his favorite team, three times by July, but there weren't enough Yankee dates to go around.

"I'm awful glad," Casey Stengel said after the season was over, "that guy ain't pitching for the Dodgers."

"The Yankees aren't so tough," Frank said in the living room of his bright, new Stone Heights home the other evening. "All you got to do is get by Mickey Mantle and Yogi Berra. Mantle didn't hit but one home run off me, and we were ahead, 8–0, then.

"I just seem to have good luck with him. There's no way to pitch him. You just mix 'em up on him and try to keep him off balance."

Lary kept Mantle so off balance he touched him for only five of his 188 hits, or a .200 average.

Between July 1 and October 1, Lary greedily ground out seventeen victories and lost only three times. There hasn't been a finish like that in the American League since Larry MacPhail re-did the interior of the Yankee Stadium Club. There, of course, must be a secret that goes with this. A fellow's got to come up with something to convert himself from a 4–10 journeyman on July 1 to a 21–13 master on October 1.

"He came up with a knuckleball," says Jack Tighe, now his manager, then his bullpen catcher. "It gave him another pitch, which he needed bad."

"I started throwing a knuckler," Frank said, "but I'd been fooling around with it before. You know, horsing around in practice. I asked Jack one day about using it. He said okay, so I tried it out and found out I was getting out good hitters like Bobby Avila and Ted Williams with it.

"But that wasn't all it was. I wasn't as bad a pitcher as it seemed like I was. Ray Boone and Al Kaline weren't hitting and we weren't scoring any runs. They say I lost confidence in myself, but that never was so. It never got that bad. The knuckler helped my confidence, but I never got real down on myself."

Frank throws his knuckler at change-up speed. He's afraid to throw it hard, afraid he'll injure his arm. He uses a two-fingertip grip on the seam, a thing he picked up from an old pitching traveler named Earl Harrist at Buffalo.

The Larys were for many seasons the backbone of all athletic teams around Northport, just across the Warrior River from Tuscaloosa. The last undefeated high school football team featured Frank, Al and Ed in the same backfield. Frank is still known as the school's greatest punter.

Five of the boys lettered in baseball at Alabama. Ed and Al played football and Al was an all-SEC end. Ed, Al and Frank were on the baseball team together one SEC championship season. Gene came later and last season won nineteen games for Mobile with a finish similar to Frank's. Al had an off year at Tulsa, won only nine.

But the greatest of them all is Frank, runt of the Lary litter, a 26-year-old boy with the fine features of an unmarked welterweight, a knuckler and twenty-one victories.

(Frank Howard was behaving like the giant in the circus. He was tired of being pointed out and gawked at. Whatever he did, exemplary or errant, was being magnified because of his physical size and the size of the bonus he'd received when he signed as a Los Angeles Dodger.

I caught him as he left the playing field one day, and while quite polite, he looked furtively about as we began talking. He suggested we seek cover. Magazine and newspaper exploitation had left him wary.

It all worked out splendidly for him as a starter. He was "Rookie of the Year" in 1960. The rest of his story is yet to be written, but all of us know the vast potential that is there.)

★ ★

VERO BEACH, Fla.—It seems that by the time I reached Dodgertown there wasn't much left of the subject of Frank Oliver Howard. He had been picked clean as a plucked chicken by magazines, wire services and research artists of spring training. They had overlooked only the size of his shirt, the size of his hat, shoes and so on.

It seemed a suitable place to begin and I am prepared to report, after conference with the largest Los Angeles Dodger, the following haberdashery measurements:

Shoes—12E.
Shirt—17 neck, 36 sleeves.
Hat (if he wore one)—7¼.

Also, he is six feet, six and one-half inches tall and weighs 240 pounds. Since he was signed for a bonus of $108,000, a figure confirmed by Vice-President Buzzie Bavasi, that means that Howard went for $770 per pound on the open market, which is a pretty fancy figure for meat of any kind.

That covering most of Howard's statistical data, there was another side of the young man that had been preying on my mind during the week.

A week ago Sunday, Howard had missed a plane to West Palm Beach, when the Dodgers flew to play Kansas City in an exhibition game. He had returned to his motel quarters and spent a pleasant afternoon with his wife. The next day Bavasi fined him. Manager Walter Alston, who has a high combustion point, ripped him up with a few well-chosen sarcasms.

Instantly my prior impression of this human Ferdinand was shattered. This could hardly be the mannerly, yessir-nossir, shy college boy I'd read about. This sounded like a spoiled brat.

Howard was coming off the field at Holman Stadium, where the Dodgers had just played an intra-squad game. Los Angeles writers had tried to talk to him and he had fled to privacy.

He was a tenderfoot at public relations. Controversy was new to him. He wasn't sure how to handle himself under fire. Now, though, the heat was off. He stopped to talk.

"Let's walk to the clubhouse," he said. "We can talk while we're walking."

Alston said Howard had been swinging too hard, and at too many bad pitches, missing big and should oughta learn the strike zone.

Was this all a product of the big press he'd drawn during the winter? Was he trying too hard to become everything they'd said he'd be all in one spring?

"When you're used to swinging one way it's hard to change," Howard said. "I just naturally swing hard. When I try to cut down on it, it does something to my timing. I think that's it, not the pressure."

Did he have any personal deadline for making good in the majors?

"I can't give you any idea how long it will take me," he said. "Of course I want to play in the majors as soon as I can. I've got to play my way up. Nobody can write me into the big leagues."

About the incident that brought on the fine . . .

"I've had family troubles," he said. "My wife has been sick. It was all just a mistake." He didn't want to talk any more on that subject.

At least two Los Angeles writers insist that Howard has acted "like a big baby" through the period of grievance. He was quoted as saying, "How can I make the team if I don't get to play?" which didn't seem to have a lot of bearing on the case.

This caused Alston to break out with a fever. "He got smart," Alston said. "He goes to the batting cage and hits fifteen more times than anybody else. He plays in eight of our first twelve games. I've spent more time with him personally than any other player in camp.

"Then he says he's mistreated.

"The trouble is, he's trying to hit those 600-foot homers. I'd rather he'd hit two 300-footers."

Wally Moon, a veteran with a cool head, said he thought Howard was still the same kid he was when he came here.

"He missed a plane. Some of the rest of us missed planes, too." Moon laughed. "I missed one, too. But then he didn't come on out to the field and work out with one of the minor league clubs. That's what burned 'em up.

"But he's a kid trying to grow up. He's got all this publicity and he's self-conscious about it. He's trying to be himself and having a hard time of it. He's no spoiled brat, though."

In that intra-squad game, Howard was given a go at third base. He played it deep and Moon laid down a bunt that no career third baseman in the world could have handled. Howard humbly approached the mound apologizing profusely to the pitcher.

That afternoon he spent thirty minutes in right field while

Alston sprayed the area with ground balls. When he swings he resembles a helicopter revved up, and when he meets the ball he drives it a great distance with mystifying ease.

He still appears out of place on a baseball field, like a giraffe dressed for a masquerade. But he is still the big attraction when the Dodgers go on the road; everything stops when he steps in the batting cage. And he still appears to be the same courteous young man he was, once-stung and wary, a-tremble at controversy and deathly fearful of reading his own statements.

SECOND CHANCE

(Selected for "Best Sports Stories of the Year.")

(June, 1961)

(There will be a shortage of readers who remember Max Lanier as the best left-handed pitcher of his day in the National League. This is because the fame he could have had was only partially developed when, as we used to say on the rural route, he "lit out" for Mexico and a false Utopia in the season of 1946.

Such an impetuous act was taken hard in Denton, North Carolina, his hometown and my hometown. We had grown up there, indulged in the same schoolboy games, played on the same high school basketball team and taken a few summer excursions together.

It was my feeling that he had short-changed not only himself, but his hometown when he ran out on the stature he was acquiring as a St. Louis Cardinal. Now, here comes another generation of Laniers with a second chance and a kind of financial stake the old man never had.)

Almost before the signatures were dry on Harold Lanier's diploma, and before he had a chance to go out and meet the world halfway, the blooming world rushed in to smother him in munificent embrace last week. This 18-year-old member of the senior class at Boca Ciega, a high school at St. Petersburg Beach, Florida, was pledged to dedicate his professional baseball services to the San Francisco Giants for a sum of $90,000.

This is of more than passing personal interest, for it was only twenty-seven years and two months ago, give or take a few days, that his daddy signed a contract with the St. Louis Cardinals for $89,900 less.

If, then, we are to assume that money is a true measure of all things, then young Harold Lanier is 900 times the player Max Lanier was. Or else baseball is simply 900 times goofier than it was twenty-seven years and two months ago.

It was a day rich in news in Denton, North Carolina, when Max Lanier was signed for the major leagues. It was some time in April. He was a senior, with graduation near, but there were no rules requiring observance of the diploma deadline in those days.

After Lanier beat Pilot High School that day, Frank Rickey displayed the delirious generosity of the Cardinals, then at the height of their chain-gang farm prosperity. He offered Lanier $100 and a bird dog to assign his left-handed self to the Cardinals.

Max lived on a farm just a short distance from town. He was accustomed to pitching hay, milking cows, drawing water from a well, manually spreading humus and other fertilizing matter, and occasionally sneaking away for some recreation in the nearby pasture, where third base was not always what it seemed to be.

To him, $100 looked like a lifetime fortune.

Frank Rickey was a kindly old man, a good salesman, as was the No. 1 Rickey, Branch. He drove Max to the farm, helped milk the cows, told folksy stories and got the old man's signature on the boy's contract and took him away.

In time, Max Lanier was to become a stout and reliable pitcher, particularly feared in Brooklyn. As a Cardinal, the public announcement that Lanier was to face the Dodgers set Flatbush to quivering.

He was broad, stubby and plump, with arms that barely reached his belt line. "You don't see good pitchers with short arms," Branch Rickey once said. "Lanier was the best short-armed pitcher I ever saw, and the best left-handed pitcher of his time in the National League."

But his launching into professionalism was something less

than spectacular. After about one month with the Greensboro, (N.C.) farm club, the record showed that Lanier had pitched in two games, retired one batter and had constructed an earned run average of 81.00.

When it was suggested that he might better prepare himself for the future at Huntington, West Virginia, Martinsville, Virginia, or Albany, Georgia, he packed up and went back to the farm. It was three years before he had a stomach for the professional stuff again, and then only because he was moving so rapidly in a semipro league that the Cardinals trapped him by flashing money.

After he advanced to the Cardinal varsity, a transition that took place in two years, money seemed to become an awful bother to him. It eventually led to the most disastrous bump in his career.

As the 1946 season began, and the Cardinals headed for the World Series, Lanier was pitching with the deft touch of a master craftsman. Nobody could beat him. They could barely score on him.

He had won six games without defeat, when upon the scene came persuasive agents from the Pasquel brothers, who were organizing their own baseball league in Mexico. They were several strides ahead of the Continental League. They simply stalked in and got what they wanted, for a price, of course.

They went to Lanier's weakness. They influenced him with money. "They poured a pile of greenbacks on the bed in New York," Ernie White, his roommate, once told me, "that had to be $75,000."

Here is where baseball management reveals itself in its ridiculous extremes. Sam Breadon, who pinched pennies, paid Lanier only $8,000 in salary though he had been a 15- and 17-game winner for him and now could assure him another pennant.

There was no question with Lanier. Go with the money, which he did, and a major league career that was approaching greatness was squandered in the dust of former bull rings and before eyes of bearded, stony-eyed pesanos who sat and watched, wearing side-arms.

Lanier came back, after four seasons on the rack, and pitched again for the Cardinals and the Giants, but the elastic had worn thin in his arms. He'd left the best of himself in Mexico, and in tank-town ball parks he'd visited as a blacklisted wanderer.

Now the Laniers get a second chance, something rare among baseball families. The son, a shortstop, catcher or pitcher, begins on a Giant farm in Quincy, Illinois, with a stake larger than his daddy earned for winning 101 games as a Cardinal, and his daddy's humbling experience to guide him.

The lesson is free of charge. The $90,000 is to keep his mind on baseball and off money.

Some ... After the Parade Had Passed

A PLAIN AND SIMPLE MAN

(December, 1951)

(*Shoeless Joe Jackson had died in Greenville, South Carolina, bringing back memories of some days we had spent together preparing his side of the Black Sox Scandal story for* Sport *Magazine.*

He patiently denied his guilt. He used his record in the series as evidence in his behalf. He was resigned now to eternal condemnation, and most of the bitterness appeared to have been dispelled.

He took me to the garage in the backyard of the modest little home. He reached up on a rack and took down a black baseball bat with a crooked handle.

"That's my old Back Betsy," he said proudly, and he took a stiff, senile stance, the old weapon cocked.

He softened me up. I left there with confused emotions. I was sure of one thing, whatever he had done, he had rationalized his innocence in his own mind.)

★ ★

Shoeless Joe Jackson was a plain and simple man who thought in plain and simple ways. He stood out from his kind only by a remarkable athletic instinct, and an extra sense that made him one of baseball's great hitters. They say he was the greatest natural hitter that ever lived.

But without a bat in his hands, he had a weakness. He relied heavily on his friends for mental guidance. Any person kind to him got in return warmth and trust, and it has since been proven that Joe's trust was in bad hands.

I'm sure that he went to his death the other night in Greenville, South Carolina, still clear of conscience. I'm sure that when and if he did accept a spot of cash for an intended part in fixing the scandalous World Series of 1919 between his Chicago White Sox and the Cincinnati Reds he did so without realizing that he was committing a wrong. He was that simple a man, and that trusting in the teammates he thought he knew so well.

I know his own story because I spent several days with him a couple of years ago recording it for a magazine. It was published "by Joe Jackson as told to," etc., though Joe to his death had never learned to read or write.

He began in plain and simple manner one August day as we sat under a small tree on the lawn of his neat little home.

"I'm not what you call a Christian," he said, "but I believe in that Good Book. What you sow, so shall you reap. I asked the Lord for guidance and I'm sure he gave it to me.

"Baseball failed to keep faith with me. When I got notice of my suspension, three days before the 1920 season ended, it said that if I was found innocent, I would be reinstated. If found guilty, I would be banned for life.

"I was found innocent. I walked out of Judge Dever's courtroom in Chicago in 1921 a free man. I had been acquitted by a twelve-man jury in a civil court. I thought when my trial was over Judge Landis would restore me to good standing. But he never did. And to this day I have never gone before him, sent a representative before him, or placed any written matter before him pleading my case. I gave baseball my best, and if the game didn't care enough to see me get a square deal, then I wouldn't go out of my way to get back in it.

"It was never explained to me officially, but I was told that Judge Landis said I was banned because of the company I kept. I roomed with Claude Williams the pitcher, one of the ringleaders, they told me, and one of the eight players banned. But I had to take whoever they assigned with me on the road. I had no power over that."

Didn't he know something was going on?

"Sure I'd heard talk. I even had a fellow come to me one day and proposition me. It was on the sixteenth floor of a hotel and there were four other people there, two men and their wives. I told him, 'Why, you cheap so-and-so, either me or you one is going out that window!' I started for him, but he ran and I never saw him again.

"I even went to Mr. Charles Comiskey (White Sox owner) before the World Series and asked him to keep me out of the lineup. He refused and I begged him to tell the newspapers he suspended me for being drunk, or anything, but leave me out of the series and then there could be no question.

"I went out and played my heart out against Cincinnati. I set a record that still stands for the most hits in a series. It has been tied, I think. I made thirteen hits, but after all the trouble came out they took one away from me. Maurice Rath went over in the hole and knocked down a hot grounder, but he couldn't make a throw on it. They scored it a hit then, but changed it later. I led both teams in hitting with .375. I hit our only home run of the series. I handled thirty balls without an error. I came all the way home from first and scored the winning run in a 5–4 game.

"That's my record in the series, and I was responsible only for Joe Jackson. There was just one thing that didn't seem quite right now as I think back over it. Eddie Cicotte seemed to let up on a pitch to Pat Duncan and Pat hit it over my head. Duncan didn't have enough power to hit the ball that far if Cicotte had been bearing down."

Joe strengthened his case of conscience by pointing to the good fortune that followed him after his banishment.

"Everything I touched seemed to turn out good for me. I've got a nice home and a seventeen-acre farm. See that lot across the street over there? I paid $240 for it and sold it for $800 in twenty-four hours."

What you sow, so shall you reap. . . .

Joe always did say that "Say it ain't so, Joe" story was a hoax. He charged it to a Chicago sports writer named Charley Owens, who at least must be given a stout hurrah for his imagination.

"It was supposed to have happened the day I was arrested in September, 1920, when I came out of the courtroom hearing. There weren't any words passed between anybody, except me and a deputy sheriff. He asked for a ride to the Southside and we got into the car together and left. Charley Owens just made up a good story and wrote it. Oh, I'd have said it wasn't so, all right, just like I'm saying it now."

Joe lived his last years in quiet and comfort, a man who dressed well, drove a Packard and doted on the respect of his South Carolina neighbors. It is perhaps odd, but when he died he was chairman of the protest committee of a semipro league around Greenville. Someone else was always delegated to read the protests and write the committee reports, it should be added.

To Joe, this was equal to exoneration. The people who knew him longest and best felt he was morally innocent. I'm sure he went with a clear conscience.

RUDY YORK: NO REGRETS

(April, 1954)

*(Rudy York is back in the major leagues now as a coach with the
Boston Red Sox. At this time, though, he was very much on the ragged
fringe. He was buried away out of sight and out of mind until some
jokester reminded a listening party that he had once led the major
leagues in arson.*

*Rudy simply had a habit of going to bed with a lighted cigar in his
face, which is not recommended for a restful night.*

*Downtown in Cartersville, Georgia, the Bartow County seat, the police
chief said Rudy had been behaving himself rather nicely. "Don't have
him down here nearly as much as we used to," he said.*

*He had a son who appeared to have some of the family hitting
ability, and watching the son had taken away some of his hell-raising
time. The son never got to the major leagues. He became a peaceful
and contented sheet-metal worker and lives a quiet life. But the old
man, he made it back to the majors, a testimonial to his persevering
ways.)*

Sometimes when I read of a young blacksmith who's clubbing
the ball a mile in spring training, but fielding as if he's got a
safe on his back, I almost always think about Rudy York. What
I mean is, I wonder about him up there in Cartersville, and what
he's doing, and if he isn't a pretty lonely guy, and if he wouldn't
like to remodel some of his past.

And so I showed up there one day, drove into his backyard

and he came out and sat down in the car and we talked awhile. He was looking pretty shapely, which was good. For a spell there he was down to about 155 pounds, which on the big York frame was nothing but hide and bone and not much tallow. He was back up to 195 this time, and he had that keen Indian look in his eyes.

"They say in that record book that I'm Indian-Irish," he said, "but there's durn little Irish in me. I'm a Cherokee Indian, and I'm proud of it. Of course when I was in the big leagues, that didn't help me out much. Any time an Indian puts on a baseball uniform he's about six times as interesting a character as the other fellow."

There's a long slice on his left cheek.

"See that scar on my face? I guess everybody figured I got that in a brawl, and that made 'em think I was rough and tough. I got that when I was nine years old. My brother was chopping wood one day and I ran right under the axe just as he swung back to chop."

For the fresh meat in the audience, Rudolph Preston York played thirteen years of major league baseball at Detroit, Boston, Chicago and Philadelphia in the American League. Eventually, he became a first baseman, but this was only after several years of attempting every position that a big fellow with a good arm, strong chest and not too much finesse can play. He gave the ball a good ride, hit 277 home runs, eighteen of them in August, 1937, which is more homers than anybody ever hit in one month in the majors.

"August always was my month," he said, chuckling and thinking kindly of the pitchers he'd tormented. "I could hit anything they'd throw at me in August, golf ball or tennis ball."

When the end came, it came suddenly. After the 1948 season with the Athletics, he got a letter in the mail that announced his unconditional release. He was only 35 years old, but he's never been in a big league suit since.

"I've got no kicks, though," he said. "I'm not the pinch-hitting kind, anyway, like Johnny Mize. I couldn't ride that bench, then go up cold and hit like he could. I don't hold anything against baseball. It was good to me. It was my ticket out of the mill town. It was my education.

"Man, I saw the sights. I'll never forget the first time I saw Yankee Stadium. I said to Charlie Gehringer, 'They don't play baseball here, do they? It's too big.' You can imagine what it was like the first time I saw a subway. I thought they'd run right out from under the ground."

If there's anything that aroused the Indian in York, it was the way the journalists slandered his fielding. Part Indian, part first baseman, they called him. "I know fielding records will fool you. I led the American League in catching in 1938, and I'd be the last guy in the world to claim I was a good catcher. If they'd have let me wear that mask out in left field, I might have been a good outfielder.

"But I never was as bad a fielder as they claimed I was at first. You know yourself it's tough for a right-hander to make the throw to second. Well, I still hold the major league record for starting double plays. I never did need any assistant out there."

For a fellow who drew around $200,000 for thirteen years' work, the big Indian hasn't got much to show for it but a nice home on the fringe of Cartersville, almost in view of the Atco mill where he once worked. He's working for about $150 a month, fighting fires for the Georgia State Forestry Commission. This should activate the good humor gland of the authors who claimed that he led the major leagues in arson, a charge growing out of a careless habit of smoking in bed.

"I needed an advisor, like that fellow who looked after Babe Ruth's money. But I didn't know who to trust. I never had had anything, though, and when I got hold of money I spent it for things me and my family had never had. I never did invest any of it. I just put it in on checking account, and that's too easy to get to.

"But I don't have any regrets. I made my mistakes. I knew I had my release coming after that season at Philadelphia. When you don't play in but thirty games and hit but .150, you can't expect much more.

"I don't miss baseball too much. I miss a lot of the guys I used to know. They don't come around any more. I never spent much time making friends, but still I don't think I've got an enemy in the world, guys I played with or against.

"Like I say, I've not got any regrets, except I wish I'd saved my money. I've had my picture on Wheaties signs as big as the side of a house. I've been in headlines on the front page. I've had kids chasing me for autographs. It was a great life. You're bound to miss it, but old Rudy ain't crying. Just think what it might have been if I couldn't play baseball."

There wasn't much else to say. He got out and told me how I should turn around and waved goodby with a magazine I'd given him. Then he went off to fight some more fires.

THE FAITHFUL RETRIEVER

(April, 1955)

(*The first morning Pete Reiser was in Thomasville, Georgia, he was startled out of his sleep by the bonging of the courthouse clock. He stayed in a restful little retreat called Rosemary Inn, nestled beneath some huge live oak trees. He walked two blocks to the bus station, where the Thomasville baseball club bus was parked, and rode to the ball park with his green kids.*

I wondered if the sedative nature of this life might not drive this tempestuous old rascal to wall-climbing or wife-beating. But it didn't. He stayed with it admirably all the way, and in time, sure enough he was back in Brooklyn.

Make that Los Angeles, if you will please.)

THOMASVILLE, Ga.—A Pittsburgh outfielder named Cully Rikard aimed a powerful drive at the center-field wall in Brooklyn one July day in 1947. Pete Reiser took out after the ball like the Crescent Limited behind schedule, and it was a run that carried him all the way from Ebbets Field to the back room at the Plaza Cafe down here in Thomasville, where of a Sunday dusk he sat passively reviewing the scars, fractures, abrasions and cheers of a baseball career remarkable in its lack of regard for major league pitchers or fences.

"Seven concussions and four fractures," said the leading example of major league surgery. "Two bad ones. The first one was in '42, chasing a ball that Enos Slaughter hit. The second one in '47 finished me off. I hit the wall at top speed. For five days they didn't know if I was going to live or die. They gave me last rites and everything. I'm lucky to be sitting here right now."

He had just arrived in Thomasville, Reiser and twenty-two young Class D Dodgers who will represent this town in the Georgia-Florida League this season. They'd spent the day on a bus from Vero Beach, Florida, where the Brooklyn baseball assembly line is located. They'd be riding that bus all summer, Pete Reiser and those among the twenty-two who can stick. And he said he's lucky to be alive.

"That's right," he said. And he told the story of some guys he knew, beanball victims and wall-crashers like himself, who were alive but would never live again. The minor league shortstop who was in a mental institution, the outfielder who had dizzy spells and had to quit, the infielder with a steel plate in his head.

"That's right," he repeated. "I'm lucky. At least I'm living."

Not so long ago he dumped his savings into a used car business that failed. Everything he'd brought out of baseball was wiped out. He wrote Walter O'Malley about returning to baseball. Early in March the president of the Dodgers called and asked how he'd like to manage the Thomasville farm club, start at the bottom, work his way up.

He'd take it, Reiser said. Lucky to be here, he said.

He talked in a monotone and shifted no emotional gears until somebody suggested that maybe he should have played the game a little less like the faithful retriever. A little cloud came over his face.

"I wouldn't have been there if I had," he said. "That's the way I played the game—all the way. I didn't know no other way. That's the way I got to Brooklyn."

That was the story of spring training, 1939, the way Pete Reiser got to Brooklyn. Judge Landis had given him and several other players freedom from the Cardinals, he'd signed a Brooklyn farm contract and been optioned to Superior, Wisconsin.

"I've been in them bus leagues before," he said. "I've made that 750-mile ride all night and all day and all the next night from Superior to Winnepeg, Canada. I know what a bus league's like."

The biggest haul he made, though, was from Superior to the Dodger training camp in '39 on the recommendation of the scout who signed him for the Cards. His first eleven times at bat Reiser reached first base on three homers, five singles and three walks. He was the sensation of the exhibition schedule. The Yankees wanted to buy him. "If they had," he said, "I'd probably still be up there. They wanted to play me at third. I wouldn't have hit them fences then."

After a stretch at Elmira, he returned to the majors to stay. In 1941, his first full season, he led the National League in all manners of hitting, including fences. This was to be his unraveling, though. He never saw the drive he could quit on, and finally he came to the end in a heap at the foot of the wall in Ebbets Field in Brooklyn.

They carried him off the field like a sack of laundry, and I see the picture yet, of some teammates walking along beside the stretcher peering hopefully into his face for some sign of life. Reiser played some more. Fact is, he was back for the World Series that year, and another season in Brooklyn, two in Boston, one at Pittsburgh and a spell with Cleveland. The Dodgers heartlessly traded him to the Braves for Mike McCormick, who wouldn't have brought the bill of his cap in Reiser's peak.

"Will you play any down here, Pete?"

George Pfister, the general manager, and Sammy Glassman, Jr., the local sports editor, both looked hopefully at him.

"We'd just like for you to be able to step up there in late innings and help out the team pinch-hitting," Pfister said, "and maybe play an inning or two in the outfield. And they've got a nice concrete fence down here for you, too."

Pete grinned. "I'm going to open on the active list. I'm going to give it a try. I had them dizzy spells down in Florida. I don't want any of that. I'll stay with it as long as I can help the team, I guess."

The main street of Thomasville was lined with bunting and

big rose-imprinted banners fluttered from the light posts as the Dodgers arrived. These were trimmings for the Rose Festival this week.

"Hum-m-m-m," Pete said as he got out of the bus and inspected his new town. "Somebody's made a mistake. They must have thought my name was Roser."

THE OBSOLETE HERO

(January, 1956)

(Dusty Rhodes didn't know it then, but he was fast going out of style. His star would never shine again. He had one more full season in the major leagues, during which he paralyzed pitchers with a harrowing .217 batting average, and then it was Phoenix, Tacoma, and other such scenic points for him.

On his visit to Atlanta the year before, I had barely been able to squeeze in a few minutes' consultation with him, so consumed was he by promotional fiends.

This time he had nothing but time, and it was friendly, casual, warming, but kind of plaintive. Somehow, neither of us felt at home without somebody tugging at Dusty's coat-tail and telling him it was time for another parade, or banquet, or to put on his television face.)

★ ★

Dusty Rhodes came back to Atlanta Thursday. This time there were no parades, no police escort, or banquets adorned by Very Important People. Dusty just delivered the body via an airline ticket registered to Rhodes, J. L., and nobody but Ed Grant paid any attention.

It wasn't because Dusty's batting average was 36 points lower, that he batted in 18 less runs, hit nine less homers or totaled 30 less bases. It was because he didn't hit a lick in the World Series, a predicament created when the New York Giants not only failed to win the pennant, but finished a bad third to Milwaukee.

"I guess you hated to see Leo Durocher go, Dusty."

"Yeah, I cried," he said, drenching friend Grant's living room with sarcasm.

"I thought Leo loved you."

"He did—as long as I was hitting," Dusty said. "You know how I'll come back to the dugout dragging my bat after I strike out? I did it in 1954. I've always done it. I struck out against Brooklyn one day and came back dragging my bat like always. Leo hollers, 'At least you can look like a ball player after you strike out!'

"I hollered back, 'What you want me to do, bust into cheers because I strike out?' You know he didn't use me again for three weeks."

The Rhodes story of the year before was something out of fantasy. The rustic Dusty had almost single-handed Cleveland out of the World Series in four games. Afterwards, there wasn't enough Rhodes to go around. Everybody wanted a piece of Dusty for a banquet, a parade, a charity, for anything. He got on a treadmill at the end of the series and didn't get off until he reported to the Giants in Arizona last March.

One of his trips was a charity adventure in Atlanta, complete with parade, banquet and much oration. The biggest affair of all came off in Rock Hill, South Carolina, where Dusty had played minor league ball and worked in a textile mill. The whole town stopped for a day while the famous pinch-hit artist returned home.

There were no parades this year, no banquets. Dusty just got off the train and he was home. You'd have thought he hit minus .017 and personally attacked Willie Mays. Actually, he didn't have a bad year. He hit .305 and drove in thirty-two runs playing mostly on call.

"I never did get myself straightened out until June," he said. "What a winter that was! Next time I'm going to go in the opposite direction of home. No more parades, no more banquets, no more of that noise.

"I got home as quiet as you please this year. I sneaked into town (Montgomery, Alabama) and nobody knew I was there.

I don't guess they cared. I've had a quiet winter. Nobody's wanted me to make any speeches or nothing. I made money last winter, but money isn't everything. Just most everything."

This trip was strictly for a visit with Grant, a native of Dusty's Alabama home region and a hunting companion of many seasons.

Dusty avoids the question of what was wrong with the Giants like the plague. "I know," he said, "but I can't say. I've got to work there again next year. I can tell you one thing:

"You read the stories about Leo resigning. Don't believe them. He never had a chance to come back. I'll bet you right now, though, that he's at Milwaukee before July next season."

Major league observers have said that Durocher's demonstrative affection for Mays created a breach that couldn't be repaired.

"I ain't saying," Dusty said. "I ain't saying a thing."

"Will you be playing regularly next season for Bill Rigney, Dusty, now that Monte Irvin is gone?"

"Horace (Stoneham) says I'll play."

"All depending on how you hit, huh?"

"No," Dusty said, coyly, "on the other." He thought that over for a moment and bounced back. "My fielding's not that bad. They talk about it, but you know how many errors I've made in two years?"

He held up two fingers. "Two," he said, "just two, and one of them I shouldn't have made."

The Giants will win the pennant by fifteen games, Dusty proclaimed, astounding his small audience. "You remember I said that," he said. "We'll win it by fifteen games, and I don't know a thing about Rigney's managing. Brooklyn will do good to finish third. Them guys are getting too old over there."

And when it happens, the Giants win it by fifteen games and Rhodes closes out another World Series in four games, don't plan any parades, banquets or speeches. Dusty won't be there. He'll be somewhere in Alaska waiting for things to cool off.

FUGATE'S DREAM

(November, 1955)

(Walter Fugate is not a famous man. He had one brief flirtation with fame, and then was hastily returned to his position in oblivion.

At the Kentucky Derby in 1950, he and his colt, a commoner named Hallieboy, harvested more press copy than any horse in Louisville before the race was run. A farmer had shown up with a plowhorse to run in this great American tradition. There hasn't been another story like it in modern Derby times.

Then there was the wrestling man who tried to buy a piece of Hallieboy the day before the Derby, and the sports writer trying to put the make on the wrestling man's private blonde, while the Fugates' little girl sang "Jesus, Lover of My Soul," backed up by a Cuban combo.

Gad, what a fantasy . . . but read on.)

A somber little man with an easy gait and some gunsmoke in his hair walked up to my desk and said: "You don't remember me, do you?"

To tell the truth, I didn't. It's a long time back to the Friday morning before the Kentucky Derby in 1950. Actually, that was the last time I'd seen Walter Fugate of Chickamauga, Georgia. The next day I had seen his Hallieboy finish tenth in a field of thirteen, and his little dream end. I hadn't realized how much of a dream was running until the owner-trainer of Hallieboy sat down the other day and talked about it again.

"If we'd only had rain that day, it would have been a different race," he said. "We'd have been up there in the purses just as sure as I'm sitting here. That Hallieboy had showed me just a week before up in Rhode Island that he purely loved the mud."

That's the beautiful part of Fugate's dream. He was a plain, simple man from a north Georgia farm. He had a plater to run in a Kentucky Derby. He still believes his plater could have won. That's the kind of dream it was.

"I'd always wanted to run a horse in the Derby," he said. "I decided to do it at the last minute, so we put Hallieboy in the trailer and drove in from Lincoln Downs. That's the way it was.

"It would have been all right if I'd have gone ahead and left right after the Derby, but I stuck around. That jock, he undone everything we'd done in the Derby. That battery thing, you know. I don't know why I rode him, anyway. I should have known better."

The jockey was a boy named George Atkins, out of Cincinnati. Within the week after the Derby he was detected giving Hallieboy electrical encouragement in a race at Churchill Downs. He was set down indefinitely and hasn't been reinstated yet.

"He could have been back by now if he'd have acted right," Fugate said. "They usually wait a year or so and let them come back. Only two jockeys I ever knew of to get set down for life. One was Don Meade and one is George Atkins.

"I remember he said to me, 'I'll be back in a year and I'll be famous.' He really had big ideas. Then he got in trouble in New Orleans. Some guy opened a hotel room door and shot his guts out. George had touted him and the guy had lost a load. He got in a fight with a guard at Louisville. He's got so much against him he's through. He fixed me, too, undone all we'd done with Hallieboy."

Fugate has a stable of ten horses now. He raced all summer at the four tracks around Cleveland. He had one good winner named Monteara, half-brother to Hallieboy. Monteara won thirty-nine races and $10,000 to $15,000 a year before he sold him. Monteara had been known to do a 2:05 mile and a quarter over the Churchill Downs course.

"But he was raced out," Fugate said. "I sold him at the right time. He was seven years old, just a plater.

"Hallieboy? Oh, I sold him a long time ago. He was claimed three or four times after that. He broke his leg and had to be shot. I missed the boat on him, though."

This goes back to the Friday morning before the 1950 Derby. There was a preposterous little drama that developed in the Mirror Room of the Kentucky Hotel with an incongruous cast. It consisted of this plain man from Chickamauga, Georgia, his wife and little girl, the sultan of female wrestling, Billy Wolfe, a flashy blonde girl wrestler, a Yankee sports writer more concerned with the blonde than the drama, and a three-piece Cuban combo.

Wolfe was trying to buy a piece of Hallieboy, whose publicity had spread like a case of itch. Fugate liked the price, but he had that dream. In the course of the dickering there came one bit of human relief. Learning that the Fugates' little girl could sing, Wolfe tried the family approach. He insisted she sing.

And so to the uncertain accompaniment of this Cuban rhumba band, feeling its way through "Jesus, Lover of My Soul," the little girl sang.

"I made my worst mistake there," Fugate said. "We were talking about $15,000 for half interest in Hallieboy. It was the big deal I should have made. If I'd a-took it, I'd have had some good backing for the future. As it was, I finally sold Hallieboy for $7,500.

"He was some feller, that Wolfe. Diamonds all over him. That three-piece Cuban band following him everywhere he went. And that blonde wrestler. She was some looker, she was. I'd be sitting pretty today if I'd made that deal. Wolfe gave me his telephone number and told me to call him if I ever got a mind to. I never did call him.

"I tell you, though, I was there to run. Then we got all that publicity, more than I ever dreamed about. But we stayed a couple of weeks too long and it was all undone. If we'd only had a wet track that day, it would have been a different story. Just as sure as I'm sitting here."

It wasn't a wet track and he did stay too long, but he's got his mileage out of the dream.

OLD GRAD FROM SOUTH BEND

(November, 1957)

(This was Johnny Lujack, one of Notre Dame's great quarterbacks, in the early stages of sunset. His name had already begun to lose its flavor, as evidenced by his report on royalties. Without that blessing of immortality, the athletic star is a most perishable product.

Lujack had come to Atlanta to appear before The Quarterback Club, whose kind are more numerous in the South than KKK Klaverns ever were. Such football societies, in fact, are standard equipment in most of the South, where the game has succeeded baseball as the national pastime. Without his radio-television exposure, Lujack would never have been here. He would have been lost among the small army of quarterbacks that graduates from college each year.)

★ ★

Johnny Lujack, who is remembered with favor at Notre Dame, was laid out on Doc Jarvis' rubbing table like a beef ready for butchering. The little maestro of the antiseptic second deck at Atlanta Athletic Club sized up his new client and lay into him with fingers that are trained to speak the language of muscles.

The client grunted some and grinned some, like a tomcat having his back scratched, and in his face seemed to be reflected all the joy of a Notre Dame man in one of his most desirable weeks.

Only last weekend Notre Dame had divorced Oklahoma from the longest winning streak in college football, even to the extreme of a shutout. In olden times, other people's winning streaks meant nothing to Notre Dame. They had some of their own, and they lived proudly.

It took only the season of 1956, spent mostly in defeat, to give the people in South Bend a new appreciation for the simpler things of life, such as calisthenics performed in unison, the lovely renditions of the band at halftime, the stirring view of the sun as it sets behind the rim of the stadium.

"That's enough," said John Lujack, who was at South Bend at a time when association with defeat was outlawed. "I'll talk.

"Yes, it hurt me last season, hurt my pride. It hurts me to lose, but most of all about last year, it hurt me to read that Notre Dame was an 18-point underdog, and that the team wasn't blocking or tackling. That didn't sound like a Notre Dame team.

"What happened between last year and this year, I'll never know. But I've got a good idea. A long winter is what happened. Those players had a long time to hear about themselves and read about it. They didn't just improve because of one year. Something else had to happen."

In his day and time, Lujack has been as superb as a quarterback can be, first in college, then as a Chicago Bear. His name became a business in itself, and he sold it to a sporting goods house for commercial purposes.

"Now," he said, "that's in its last stage. I got a notice the other day that I had some royalties coming. Know how much they were? Nine dollars.

"That's a real comedown. My first year I drew $14,000 in royalties on equipment they sold using my name. Your name, I've found out, is only as good as what you're doing with it on the field."

From "back of the year" in '47 to all-pro in '50, the course has led to the broadcast booth. Last season Lujack worked the NCAA telecasts and thus was spared visual suffering at Notre Dame's bedside. This year he broadcasts Green Bay Packer games and has come to view with alarm the come-uppance suffered by his last alma mater, George Halas U.

"The Bears have got some of the greatest talent in football," he said. "There's not a finer end in football than Harlon Hill. He's a genius to watch. He'll make you smile just looking at him get out and downfield."

The natural target for Bear investigators is inside the coaches' office. Paddy Driscoll is the head coach by the roster, but it is said that Halas still runs the team. Whoever it is, as Lujack sees it, that doesn't make a lot of difference.

"The head coach in pro ball is not nearly as important as the college head coach," he said. "It's up to his assistants to stay close to the players. The head coach is more like an office manager. He coordinates things.

"Maybe it is the coaching, but that doesn't necessarily mean the head coach. A lot of these pro coaches will work their men day and night, two-hour workouts by day, meetings at night. They forget players have families at home. The wife may be upset. A kid may be sick. You can't regiment the pros like you do the college boys.

"We went into New York once and we'd got sick of meetings and routine, so we decided to stay out all night. I didn't get in until seven o'clock in the morning. I got three hours sleep. Then we went out and beat the New York Yanks, 52–21. I couldn't throw a pass that didn't get caught. One of our defensive ends, Ed Sprinkle, even caught one, in George Taliaferro's territory. It made Taliaferro so mad he threw his helmet down and walked off the field.

"The only receiver that dropped a pass that day was an end named John Hoffman. He was also the only guy who went to bed at curfew."

THE STUBBORN HOOSIER

(March, 1958)

(*I walked into the press room at Bradenton, Florida, one spring day and this took place. All I did was mention holding out to Edd Roush, then let Warren Spahn and Ed Mathews take over the cross-examination.*

Sometimes columns come off best this way. The less you talk, the more you learn, my mother used to say. So I kept quiet and listened. There was only one handicap here. It's mighty difficult trying to make notes and eat a Dagwood sandwich at the same time.)

BRADENTON, Fla.—Some of the Milwaukee Braves, tres-passing in the press room the other day, found Edd Roush engaged in a construction project. He was building a sandwich consisting of several slices of bologna and Swiss cheese surrounded by two slabs of rye bread, after which he collapsed on a divan and began a vigorous attack with his teeth.

"Say, Edd," said Warren Spahn, revealing an ancient historian's knowledge of baseball, "why did you hold out back there in 1929, or '30, or whenever it was?"

"Thirty," Edd said.

He finished chewing a hunk of sandwich, then wiped his mouth with the back of a sun-bronzed hand.

"John McGraw had paid me $25,000 in 1929 and I'd hit .324," Roush said. "He wanted to cut me to $15,000. I told him

I'd quit first. I was thirty-seven years old, anyway, and I knew I was about through. I didn't see any sense in going back to play another year for a $10,000 cut after the record I'd had."

What took place was the most stubborn holdout the National League ever saw. That fall, and into the next spring Roush was still holding out. He missed the entire season with the Giants and had no intention of ever playing again.

"The next winter I got a telephone call from Tampa. It was Sid Weill, who owned the Cincinnati ball club and was about to go broke. He wanted to know if I'd play for the Reds. I told him why I wouldn't play for the Giants and he said he'd gotten permission from McGraw to talk to me and that Cincinnati could have me for the waiver price if I'd play.

"I told Weill then that I was about thirty-eight years old and I wouldn't be worth it to him. He insisted. He told me to name my price. I just told him I'd think it over awhile."

In Cincinnati the name of Roush was sacred. He had played eleven seasons there and ten of them he had hit .321 or better. Twice he led the National League in batting. Today he still stands one-two in every Cincinnati offensive record except for the power department. In 1927 he had been traded to the Giants.

"A few weeks later Weill called again. He said he would be coming up my way—I live in Oakland City, Indiana—and he'd like to meet me in Indianapolis. I told him again that I thought I was through, but I met him anyway.

"I told him I'd play for him for $15,000, but 'I think you're crazy to pay it,' I said. He arranged the deal and I reported to the ball club ten days before the season opened. I met the team in Birmingham. I never did need no spring training anyway.

"Well, I was right. I played in about 100 games and I think I hit about .270. I was through, all right, and I showed it. I was sorry to take Weill's money, because he needed it. It wasn't long before he sold out to Larry MacPhail."

"That $25,000 that McGraw paid you in 1930, though, wasn't it worth about what $100,000 would be today?" Spahn asked.

"Yeah," Roush said. "It was mighty good pay. McGraw said

the reason he cut me was because of the depression and he knew like I did that I was through. Salaries never would have been anything in the majors if it hadn't been for the Federal League. That threw a scare into the majors back about '15 and they jacked up the pay some."

"What was an average salary for a rookie back in your time?" Ed Mathews asked.

"Oh, around $2,500," Roush said. "Some would make as high as $3,000, but $2,500 was about the average."

Mathews' lower lip fell. "Twenty-five hundred?" he said.

"Yeah, son, that was back before they started paying for the home run. Now everybody tries to hit home runs like you do to get the big pay. The season right after I left Cincinnati they moved the plate out about 125 feet. That's how big the ball park was."

"Edd, didn't you regret that you laid out that season?" Spahn asked. "Don't you think you might have lasted longer if you'd have kept playing?"

"I don't regret it a bit. I was up there seventeen years. Not many fellers ever played longer than that. If you know yourself when you're through I think it's better than somebody having to break the news to you."

"What did you do the year you held out?"

"Nothing," Roush said. "Hunted and fished. That's all I've done in my life, hunted and fished and played baseball. Lived all my life in Oakland City, except when I come down here in January every year."

"Why is it," asked another member of the party, "you come down here every spring now and when you played you tried to miss all of spring training you could?"

"I was always in shape. That's why. Nobody ever had to drive me around like I was cattle to get me ready to play ball. I knew when I was ready to play and I knew when I wasn't."

You don't argue the point with a fellow whose lifetime batting average was .323 and who was stubborner than John McGraw.

THE DESTITUTE SLUGGER

(Selected for "Best Sports Stories of the Year.")

(January, 1959)

(*As a cub reporter, I remember driving to Greensboro, North Carolina, to see the Boston Red Sox play the Cincinnati Reds in a spring exhibition game. A Cincinnati catcher named Willard Hershberger hit three home runs and a ground-rule double. Later that season, Hershberger killed himself in his hotel room in Boston in a state of despondency brought on by play that he felt let his teammates down.*

Another player on the way to a human tragedy, but unaware of it that day, was the stalwart first baseman of the Red Sox, Jimmy Foxx. Never had I seen so impressive a physical figure, his sleeves cut back to allow his massive biceps to have their play.

Most of a great career was behind him, but there was no cause to suspect that Jimmy Foxx would ever see a day of want. And yet, here we have him, reduced to a human refugee, trying to hide from himself. It is hard to find any pity for him.)

By this time, Jimmy Foxx has been rescued from destitution and awarded gainful employment. He was caught up in a tidal wave of public pity and washed ashore at Minneapolis, where he will be the coach on Manager Gene Mauch's staff next season.

This was the Boston Red Sox' manner of providing for a former loyal servant. The charitable theory was that the world had dealt unfairly with the second most productive home run hitter of all time and that something should be done to make up for the slight.

For several years, Foxx was out yonder in nowhere. Baseball had quit keeping a book on him. But he'd also quit keeping a book on himself. He was merely riding along with the current and the current was moving downstream.

What brought him out of self-stagnation was a simple little incident involving an invitation to a sports writers' dinner in Boston, where he lived his richest days. Foxx turned down the invitation, explaining that he couldn't afford plane fare.

It was the most profitable confession he ever made. For the next few days the world fell all over itself trying to volunteer its services in his behalf. He became a television star. He was invited to write a book. He was offered a lifetime supply of dinosaurburgers. People sent him money and promises of money. Everybody was saying the major league pension plan ought to be revised to take care of him. Whitlow Wyatt has been saying all the time that it ought to be revised to take care of players like Foxx and Wyatt. Both missed it by a year.

Everybody, though, was coming out with a Jimmy Foxx Plan, Trust funds, job offers, scholarships to correspondence schools, and there seemed to be no limit to his future. Life was beginning for him again at 50.

Now, let's look at the case from a purely unemotional point of view.

James Emory Foxx in his burliest days was known as the "Maryland Strong Boy." He played ten seasons with the Philadelphia Athletics when they were virile. He played seven with the Red Sox, two with the Chicago Cubs and one lame duck season with the Phillies.

He hit 534 home runs, including 58 in 1932, when it looked sure as thunder as if he'd tie Babe Ruth's record of 60. That is the major league record only. The all-time record is 72, struck by Joe Baumann of Roswell, New Mexico, three years ago.

Baumann made $500 per month, bought himself a filling station and is providing for his family nicely if not elegantly. Foxx made $270,000, he estimates, and hasn't a dime to show for it.

This kind of prodigality usually is associated with alcoholism and wild living. Foxx was neither alcoholic nor a playboy, though it is understood that in recent years whisky did become a problem as he applied himself rather diligently to attempts at drowning his sorrow.

Foxx seems to have been badly advised and a poor business-man both, which is a double-barreled cinch to blow a stake. He invested a pile of dough in a golf club at St. Petersburg, Florida, just before the war and lost it all. That made the next step in his personal depression that much easier and he became a natural attraction for reverses.

This kind of human despondency is totally out of character with the Foxx you remember as a player. I got my first view of him as the Boston first baseman in 1939. The Red Sox stopped in North Carolina for an exhibition game on the way north.

It was a spring day with a nip in it, but Foxx was a manly sight. He had forearms like entwined hawsers. He had biceps like knots in an ancient oak. And he wore his sleeves cut short for all to see. I'll never forget what an impressive brute of a man he was. He looked like he could play forever, though he had only three more good seasons left.

What seemed to have happened to Foxx was a failure to re-adjust to life off the stage, out of range of the cheers and the adulation. This is an occupational hazard. Some survive it and some don't.

But this kind of thing comes up frequently, the old hero down and out and the worshipful public rallying to the wall. Some-how, I fail to respond to the cry that baseball and the world has a debt to Jimmy Foxx. It paid him handsomely while he per-formed. It offered him opportunities after he could play no longer.

He was a failure as a manager. He walked out on a job as coach of the Miami Marlins. He sat down and waited for the world to come hammering on his door. And while he waited he tried to forget that he had been forgotten.

He did so well at it that he almost forgot a man must work to live. And it is hard to sell those of the unemotional point of view the story that there is no employment available for a 220-pound figure of a man in good health, and with forearms like entwined hawsers and biceps of knotty oak.

Some Events to Remember

THE FIGHTING VICE-PRESIDENT

(August, 1957)

*(This was one of the most weird adventures in the history of sport.
Pete Rademacher, a former soldier and Olympic heavyweight boxing
champion, had turned professional by fighting Floyd Patterson for the
world championship.*

*It was all the promotion of the victim himself, Heavyweight Rade-
macher, who was a splendid salesman. He was cultured, articulate,
persistent and confident as hell, but only an average fighter.*

*This was the one brief moment when he allowed his guard to fall, when
he was overwhelmed by the emotion of it all. The fight was just over.
There would never be another moment like this for the vice-president
of Youth Unlimited. He had started at the top and could only expect
to work his way down.*

*One thing about the fellow, you had to like him. As much as anything
else, I admired him.)*

SEATTLE—A degree of calm had settled over the dressing
room of the challenger. The size of the writhing mob had
dwindled. The television cameras had finished their grinding
and the garish floodlights had been retired. Pete Rademacher, a
man with a broken dream, slipped off the table of inquisition
and walked toward the shower room, followed by his trainer,
George Chemeres, and his pal, Joe Gannon.

He stripped down to the raw 202 pounds marked only by a
trace of blackened eye and started to step under a shower. But

a heavy wave of emotion wrenched him and he burst into a convulsion of sobs.

This lasted for about a minute, while Chemeres and Gannon stood by helplessly. Then Rademacher, who had not won the heavyweight championship of the world from Floyd Patterson, stepped under the shower.

"All that tension and pressure," Chemeres said, "he had to give some place. He's been carrying an awful big load."

So the tears were not of remorse or bitterness. Merely the escape valve of emotion. There were no tears to be shed for the performance.

For 15 minutes and 57 seconds, Rademacher had given it his best riffle. In three rounds, for that matter, he had won his case. Proved his point. He belonged in the same ring with the champion.

All these months, all these weeks and all these nights, by the placid waters of Lake Huston in Georgia, and in the cool highlands of Issaquah in Washington, where he had worked out the final points of his ambition, the load had been piling up.

Then at 10 o'clock sharp, Seattle time, the champion of the Olympics had heard the bell ring and he had gone out on the hunt for the holy grail. He didn't find it, but he did find a certain kind of honor.

He had stayed with the champion. He had fought him. He had knocked him to the deck. He had been knocked to the deck himself, but the aggressor had never been knocked out of him.

Cus D'Amato, the grey-haired Italian who manages Patterson, took the opportunity to sting the critics of the challenger.

"This fellow," he said, "gave us a better fight than any of those bums back East." Meaning, chiefly, Hurricane Jackson.

Chemeres, exercising the prerogative of a trainer abundant with afterthoughts, could see how it might have been. This had been his big moment, a little Greek who had drawn little water out here before, and who had been paid only passing attention before and who had gone broke trying to run fight gyms, returning with the most extraordinary challenger of all time.

"He should have unloaded on him after he got him down in the second round," he said. "If he'd have stayed in there close like he started, it would have never ended this way. He made the fight for the first three rounds, then he moved back and that was it."

The challenger, however, was a realistic loser. He'd left about everything he had in the ring. A fellow goes down seven times for a total count of seventy-three and he learns a lot of arithmetic.

"But if I could fight him again tomorrow," Rademacher said, "I'd be in there. It was a great and exciting experience. If I fought him again I guess I'd do the same thing again. I'd blow my cork."

Rademacher was not a particularly impressive boxer. Patterson spoke frequently in his crowded quarters of his "sneaky right."

"He stung me when he knocked me down," the champion said. It had looked more like a shove. "He hit me with a right to the chin. It was a knockdown. He's a little slow, but he makes up for it with that sneaky right."

It is possible that Rademacher's professional career began and ended in that same ring that straddled the pitcher's mound at Sicks Stadium. At least this would be in line with the suggestion of Tommy Loughran, who came out from New York to referee the bout.

"I don't think the boy should continue as a professional," he said. "He's too old. He has too much to learn. He can do too much better in some other field."

For one cool evening heavy with drama and the incredible, Rademacher had won honor with courage. "Sometimes," said Mike Jennings, his leading backer and president of Youth Unlimited, whose plan it is to set examples, "you can set a better example losing than you can winning. I've never been prouder of Pete than I was tonight." Friday, the directors of Youth Unlimited held a board meeting. They led with a vote of confidence for the incumbent vice president.

DEFEAT BY PROXY

(July, 1958)

(Curt Simmons had suffered the humiliation of a knock-out in the second inning of the major league All-Star game in St. Louis. Lew Burdette had walked in a run. Now they were in the clubhouse listening by radio to their last chance at redemption, which never came about.

A National League rally in the ninth inning was short. While none of this went into the season records, Simmons and Burdette both proved that winning is everything, especially in an All-Star game when performance is ordered to be its keenest.

The little human touch I liked most about this occasion was supplied by the fat clubhouse attendant, the one who said, "Me, too, Lew.")

★ ★

ST. LOUIS—"Now," Lew Burdette barked, like an irritated collie, "you see why I'm so mad about walking in that run in the second inning. We'd be tied now."

A small radio set on top of the lockers at Busch Stadium fed Harry Caray's excited voice into the National League clubhouse. Burdette of Milwaukee, who had relieved a distressed Curt Simmons of Philadelphia in the second inning, was dressed in street clothes and sat on a red stool. Larry Jackson of St. Louis, who had worked two late innings, was just coming out of the shower, a trail of drip marks in his wake. Simmons sat at the far end of the clubhouse on a table, head down, feet dangling.

He said nothing. He wanted off the hook, for he would be the losing pitcher.

Three National League runs were in in the ninth inning and

the noose was as tight as it would go around the American
League necks. Now the score was 6–5 in the major league
All-Star game, two out in the ninth and Gil Hodges of Brooklyn
batting for Clem Labine of Brooklyn.

"How much does the All-Star game mean to you fellows
now?" somebody asked Burdette.

"A helluva lot," Burdette said. "A fellow's got his pride, you
know. First, you want to get in the game then you want to
win it. It means that you're better than they are. That's what it's
all about, isn't it? To see who's the best?"

He turned back to Harry Caray. "Come on, Gil," he said.
"Lose it, man.

"I pull for this guy now," Burdette said, "but I just pull
for him this one day a year. The rest of the time I want to
beat him."

A fat clubhouse attendant turned to Burdette and laughed.
"Me, too, Lew," he said. "That's the way I am."

The place was dense with tension now. Jackson quit toweling
himself down and listened. Bob Grim of the Yankees was
pitching now . . . carefully.

Somebody cracked the top on a can of beer, speared out
of a tub of chipped ice.

"It's a line shot to left field," Caray screamed. "Right into
the hands of Minnie Minoso, and the ball game is over."

"You see," said Burdette, popping his hands on his knees,
"if I hadn't walked in that run in the second . . ."

In a few seconds there was the sound of spikes on the steps
outside. The door burst open and Ed Mathews of Milwaukee
came in first, unbuttoning his shirt as he did. Then Gus Bell
of Cincinnati and Warren Spahn of Milwaukee and Willie
Mays of the Giants and the place became a quiet but active
tomb of male strippers.

"That was the biggest curve I ever saw in my life," Mathews
said. Don Mossi of Cleveland had struck him out with two
men on in the frantic ninth. "I'd never seen him pitch before.
I didn't know he had a curve like that. I never saw one like
that before."

Bell, who had been thrown out at third on Ernie Banks' single, wasn't agitated, but he was positive. "I was safe, ask Bobby Bragan. He was right on top of it."

Bragan, the third base coach, said that was right, Bell was safe. Frank Dascoli had said he wasn't. Dascoli had got his way.

One floor below, where the American League superbs dressed, bedlam existed. Jim Bunning, the tall, lanky Detroit pitcher, was still in his uniform. He had pitched the three first innings perfectly, then stayed on the bench.

"Man, I didn't want to leave," he said. "I'd never seen an All-Star game before."

Ted Williams had been frisky as a spaniel before the game. Only once, when a father jumped the box rail with his son and approached him, did he show his other side. There was justification. In the clubhouse he was jubilant. Like the All-Star game did mean something, like Lew Burdette had said.

In a hot corner, hemmed in by sweating, pressing newspaper authors, Dr. Charles D. Stengel of the New York Yankees, observing his second All-Star victory, cheerfully gave of himself.

"What I said was," he said, and he had not been particularly joyful about starting Bunning, "that no All-Star pitcher should work for three days before the game, except in relief. This (Billy) Pierce goes great for two innings, then his arm gets tired and it won't do no more what his brain tells it to do. My boy (Grim) had not worked since the Fourth of July.

"He pitched eight strikes that day against Boston, but we needed nine. Mickey Vernon hit the other pitch for a home run and we don't win.

"So I call on him, and it's a great game. Williams swings the bat well. Berra looks good at the plate. Minoso, he's got to have the last word in the ninth inning, and it wins for us. And this, yes, Bunning, he pitches good ball. I'm going to get around to that. He does real good. It's a big game. It's a great event.

"And," he added, rolling his eyes slow like a lazy alligator, "I'm very glad the boys win it for the old man."

FRENCH ALSO FOUGHT HERE

(December, 1958)

(Television is a many-headed dragon. If you can't be there, it sometimes brings the event to you. If you are there, it sometimes sees, you learn later to your ambarrassment, more and better than you saw.

This was one of the most vivid fights I ever witnessed, consisting of two diverse sections. At one stage Archie Moore was being slaughtered. In time, Sir Archibald became the slaughterer.

I have seen several Moore fights, at ringside and at fireside. Never have I seen him come nearer achieving universal admiration than he did on this televised night in Canada.)

★ ★

There are certain hazards involved in the coverage of a prize fight by fireside, particularly at a location whose census count includes three young men ranging from diaper age to nine. And so it happened that by the time I could soothe the stomach pains of an overfed young one and return to the side of our television set Wednesday evening, the screen was already smoking with action at Montreal, P.Q., Canada.

Monsieur Archie Moore had already fallen hard three times for Yvon Durelle, who is no lady. The elderly diamond merchant for San Diego, California, was wobbling back toward his corner and he fell severely wounded to his stool.

Yvon Durelle is an humble fisherman from Baie Ste. Anne, New Brunswick, which is a Canadian state. In between catches he engages in pugilism. His distinction in the field has been limited, however. He is known chiefly for having been an eight-round victim in the Floyd Patterson preparatory campaign, and an eight-round knockout victim of Clarence Hinnant, ordinarily a kindly fellow.

Oh, in his time Durelle has won from such curious people as Billy Snowball, Cobey McCloskey, Manuel Leek, Alvin Upshaw, Coo McRae and Tinker Picot. Also, he turned the year 1957 into an outstanding campaign, winning in its course the light heavyweight title of the British Empire.

Even this and the fact that he had the Canuck world behind him, however, gave him no right at all to knock down M. Moore three times in one night, much less a round.

While busy people wearing sequined shirts that read, "Diamond Palace, San Diego," hovered over the wounded Moore, Jack Drees explained in broken English how the sponsor had been so moved by the Canuck demonstration that the leadoff commercial had been omitted. This was equally as large an upset as Moore's present condition.

Displaying remarkable recuperative powers, Moore answered the bell and spent the second round observing the fisherman's style from a distance. By the third round the big showoff was doing deep kneebends.

This was interpreted as an accommodating gesture to Durelle and all the other French-speaking members of the house that, "M. Moore est non mort." Or something like that.

It was in this round that Durelle flurried briefly and when Drees hastily pointed out that he hadn't landed a blow. "You must remember," he said, "that these cheers are from a partisan Canadian crowd." Which, he might have added, was being badly outnumbered by the television commentator.

In the fourth, Moore had returned to his original being and was fighting the cagey fight. Both he and Durelle managed to unload a few uncomplimentary blows to each other's pelt. They were so busy at work, in fact, that neither seemed to care for the sound of the bell and had to be parted by referee

Jack Sharkey, who at this time appeared to be stronger than either champion or challenger.

Now for the fifth. This was a return to drama. Durelle caught Moore with a solid right visible to every television subscriber and the huge brown body sagged by the ropes. Moore staggered back to his feet and clawed the air and Durelle's body with grasping gloves, like a drowning man making his last thresh at survival.

Suddenly this confident, scowling fellow was transformed into an old man of 43, 45 or 49. He was as aged as anyone has ever guessed, ready to be whipped to a froth.

But the sturdy fisherman was fatigued from the flailing. Not only couldn't he locate the last punch, he couldn't stay clear of Moore's frantic clutch and they remained coiled in a tangled huddle of brown and white limbs until Moore abruptly broke loose with some dynamite of his own.

This was, as they say in football, the turning point. Durelle had shot his last volley. Moore had survived it. He was now the caller of the shots.

It wasn't too long coming and in the audience the Canuck fervor, the lust for the kill was dying in the larynx. In the seventh Moore had Durelle down, in spite of his eight-inch wrists. In the tenth Durelle was down again and again, and now you remembered something he'd said before the fight.

"One of us is going to win by the eleventh or twelfth round," he'd said. "I'm going to win or be carried out."

He'd said it with clairvoyance. In the eleventh round they carried him out while the ring announcer, Pierre Something-or-another, scrambled for the microphone to deliver the sad message.

"Mesdames et messieurs," he began gravely, like DeGaulle announcing the fall of Paris. "Le gal-own champ-yon," and so forth. Moore had won in forty-nine seconds of the eleventh round.

The result had a saddening effect, too, on history in Georgia. Young Stribling's record for knockouts was dead, 127–126. Moore had outdone W. L. merely by outlasting him. W. L.

almost made a Frenchman his 126th, a fellow named Pierre Charles in Paris, March 6, 1933. But he saved it and brought it home for Benny O'Dell, and the blow was delivered at Rome August 2, a couple of months before he was killed.

Now that it's gone, they might as well make the break good and clean. Give the ageless, artistic diamond merchant credit for two this time. He had to knock out Durelle in two languages.

TRAFFIC COURT IN LOUISVILLE

(May, 1959)

(This was a moment of great tension at Churchill Downs. Winners of the Kentucky Derby are not usually determined in the office of the track stewards. You knew that no winner of such a race as this would be taken down, but at the same time you couldn't be sure.

Everybody from Willie Shoemaker to the most cautious $2 bettor with a ticket on Tomy Lee spent several minutes of agony while court was being held under the stands.

Frankly, I would have suggested that they run the race over if the stewards were not entirely satisfied with the results. After all, what could have been better than a doubleheader at the Kentucky Derby?)

LOUISVILLE—A sort of unrest prevailed in the winner's circle at Churchill Downs after the seventh race Saturday afternoon. A messenger had arrived from the steward's office and retrieved Willie Shoemaker off the back of Tomy Lee, a colt born in England, owned by a Texan, campaigned in California and now the winner of the Kentucky Derby, but charged with employing devious tactics.

Bill Boland claimed that Shoemaker and Tomy Lee had impeded his progress on Sword Dancer as they hustled down the stretch to the wire. Shoemaker, such a mere bit of human being, looked like a little boy picked up for jimmying gum machines as he was escorted across the track for the hearing, still in his white and lemon-colored silks, the messenger and reporters towering over him.

In just two minutes, two and three-fifth seconds Tomy Lee had settled the dust on a most confusing Derby situation. Of seventeen colts who made the race, all with a degree of hope, he had proven best. Now, confusion had broken out all over again.

There was a photographic finish involved, for Tomy Lee and Sword Dancer had gone to the wire whisker to whisker. But there hadn't been a great deal of doubt about what the picture would show. Tomy Lee, the inside horse, had the margin, it had seemed.

Now, though, Tomy Lee was to be presented an opportunity never before allowed the winner of a Kentucky Derby. He was invited to defend his title.

There had been a case of a contested finish back in 1880, when a colt named Fonso won the sixth Derby in a five-horse race. The book of Derby history, however, merely says this:

"Fonso broke in front and stayed there, winning by a length. Kimball was always second and Bancroft was always third. Foul claim lodged by Kimball's jockey against Fonso, not allowed."

In those days, though, the Kentucky Derby was no more than a county fair race. The total purse was only $4,000. The race was run on a track so dusty that only the leading horse could be clearly seen.

Don Meade on Broker's Tip and Herb Fisher on Head Play fought it out horse to horse down the stretch in 1933, applying the whip to each other, tugging at saddle cloths and battling on into the jockeys' room. Neither filed a claim, but the stewards hauled them both in for a paddling.

Now, Willie Shoemaker and Bill Boland were under questioning. Film patrol movies were under study. Out in the winner's circle there was nothing to do but stand a restless watch. A tall man, straight up and down, with a face of western steel and hair tinged with gray, allowed someone to put the wreath of roses around his neck. He grinned broadly. Then he removed the wreath and moved about among the crowd. He looked at his watch.

This was Fred Turner Jr., who owns Tomy Lee. He is an oil man and cattle rancher around Midland, Texas.

Someone put the wreath of roses around the neck of another old gentleman, who also grinned broadly. He had the face of a southern gentleman. With a black string tie and a white goatee he'd have looked ever so scenic standing on the porch of a Kentucky mansion, a libation in his hands.

This was Frank Childs, 71 years old, the trainer of Tomy Lee.

I remembered so well what Childs had said Thursday morning when a group of wanderers came upon him in the barn area.

"Gentlemen," he said, pointing to Tomy Lee, "you're looking at the winner of the Kentucky Derby."

Childs held the rein while Tomy Lee munched some grass in the yard. A colt standing a few feet away was Tuleg, a Tulyar son Turner had bought for $10,000 more than the price of Tomy Lee. He'd bought Tomy Lee to keep Tuleg company, and Tuleg had come up lame this year.

"What did you like about Tomy Lee when you saw him first?" a fellow asked Childs.

"Nothing," Childs said. "Calf-kneed, light-boned, surely not a horse you'd buy off his looks."

There was some smart campaigning here. Tomy Lee passed up the Santa Anita Derby and the California Derby, for one reason or another, and came early to Kentucky for the Keeneland races. This is where he made his impression on the hardboots, like Roscoe Goose, who never cares for favorites.

"This colt is coming up," Roscoe said. "Sword Dancer is coming up. Some of the others have already reached their peak. The ones that's coming up is the ones that wins the Derby."

On the little podium that overlooks the winner's circle, Gov. Happy Chandler was carrying on in traditional form. His best political smile was pasted on his face and he turned from side to side, flashing every angle for the television customers.

No winner of a Kentucky Derby would come down. You

knew it. The race had to stand. But the unrest hung on. You couldn't be sure.

There was a roar. The red "official" sign had flashed on the board. The stewards had turned down the claim. The winner was Tomy Lee. Activity was resumed in the winner's circle. Everybody moved about with purpose now. The unrest disappeared.

The prices flashed on the board and ticket-holders started for the cashiers' windows. Sword Dancer would have to wait for another chance. He'd get it in the Preakness, two weeks away. He'd win then, he surely would. And without all this unrest.

DINNER FOR 1,200 AND TWO

(July, 1959)

(*This was one of the richest, warmest moments I've ever known in sports. The Pittsburgh people had gone a little farther than most All-Star game hosts to give the annual occasion a little touch of heart.*

It looked at the time as if both Musial and Williams were through, and that this would be their last All-Star appearance. Both had been invited to this game as a matter of sentiment rather than a matter of record.

As much as anything else, it was a grand departure from convention to see Theodore Williams dressed out in a white shirt and a necktie. He had at one time sworn that he'd rather drop dead than be found in any kind of haberdashery any less comfortable than an open-necked sports shirt.)

★ ★

PITTSBURGH—Ted Williams stepped off the elevator seventeen floors above Pittsburgh Monday evening trussed up in a white shirt and a necktie, a concession this champion of the open-necked sports garment had made to a rather special occasion in his behalf and the behalf of another left-handed hitter, Stan Musial. The Pittsburgh Chapter of the Baseball Writers Association of America had rented the ballroom and several outlying rooms of the Penn-Sheraton Hotel and pioneered a new type of organized entertainment to jolly up the occasion of the twenty-sixth major league All-Star game.

The Pittsburgh entrepreneurs had chosen to dedicate the

evening to Musial and Williams, "for long and meritorious careers in baseball." But this was only a portion of a glamorous evening designed to thrill the lover of the art of baseball to the marrow of his bones.

When they marched into their seats on the dais, the stars who would play at Forbes Field, and the troupe of ancient and semi-ancient gentlemen of the game, and the national figures, you could see that more than casual planning had gone into the occasion.

Casey Stengel of the New York Yankees sat between Vice President Richard Nixon of the U.S.A. and Ben Fairless of U.S. Steel, Harvey Haddix of the twelve-inning perfect game next to Atty. Gen. William P. Rogers of the U.S.A., Fred Haney of the Milwaukee Braves next to Gov. David Lawrence of Pennsylvania, and Danny Murtaugh of the Pittsburgh Pirates next to a Catholic bishop who looked amazingly like Danny Murtaugh.

Earlier, a small, wizened man had trudged laboriously through the heavy nap of the hotel rugs on his way to the head table, moving with the insignificance of a maintenance man. Hardly any of the later generation would have suspected him of being the remains of the greatest hitter of the modern Pirates.

And this man, Paul Waner, took his seat at one end of the dais listing heavily with history, Lefty Grove, Carl Hubbell, George Sisler, Hank Greenberg, Joe Cronin, Pie Traynor, Dizzy Dean and Ralph Kiner in his vicinity.

Then George Jessel, about as tall as the battery of microphones that faced him, began to warm up the audience of 1,200.

Vice President Nixon, seasoned in this sort of function, was requested to throw out the first ball, fortunately manufactured of plastic. A lady in the back of the room caught it, whereupon Jessel attempted to reveal the name of the catcher.

"I understand the ball the Vice President just threw out was caught by Mrs. Bob Waterfield," he said.

It turned out that his identification was several inches incorrect. The catcher was Mrs. Bob Porterfield, whose husband has had limited success pitching for Pittsburgh.

"Coming to the All-Star game as a .250 hitter," Musial said, "is, uh, well, rather unusual. I feel like sneaking in through the center-field gate tomorrow.

"I'd like to say a few words about my friend, Ted Williams. We've both been having a real struggle this year, but we've been talking it over. We've both decided that we'll finish over .300."

Williams approached the lectern with the uncomfortable gestures, the shrug of the shoulders, the tug at the sleeves, the evasive eyes of a small boy about to recite at commencement. Then he looked up and he grinned a warm grin and he immediately exposed a trace of the mellowness that is possessing him.

"All the other players here tonight were voted to their positions on the All-Star teams of their respective leagues," Williams said. "I'm sorry I can't say that I was elected.

"I got two base hits Sunday afternoon, and I was awful happy to get those two hits. That used to be just another day's work for me. But I'd done some figuring.

"Two hits would give me an average of .223. That's two pounds more than I weigh, so they couldn't say I wasn't hitting my weight when I came down here."

Williams laughed and his audience laughed, and it was this kind of eye-watering sort of evening between its fits of high humor. There was nothing, though, more touching than a Musial gesture, made in the casual, unstaged manner that is his.

"I've got one particular fan in Pittsburgh I'd like to introduce," he said. "My mother's sitting over there. I wish she'd stand up and take a bow. Stand up, Mom."

Mom stood up, and she was a sweet, white-haired lady dressed as you would have your mother dress. She threw her shoulders back and a surge of pride and love for her son overwhelmed her. Tears rushed down her pale cheeks and she sat down to dab at them with her handkerchief. The audience stood with her and they cheered strong, and it was a gripping moment, as if Mrs. Musial was the representative for all mothers.

Dizzy Dean, self-appointed chairman of a one-man Committee to Improve Things for Pitchers, commiserated at some length with Harvey Haddix on the remarkable game the small left-handed Pirate pitched and lost to Milwaukee.

"There ain't no question about it," Jerome H. Dean said, "I was a pretty fair country pitcher. Well, they ain't done nothing to help them pore pitchers since I was pitching, like move the mound closer to the plate or build it bigger to hide behind. Now they've made another rule against 'em. They won't even let you throw at nobody.

"I never wanted to kill nobody. I just wanted to straighten up them batters ever once in awhile."

Well, this is the way it went for about two fast, orderly hours. Then the vice president noticed that it was about 10 o'clock, and that the athletes ought to be getting to bed. It was just getting ready to break up when Jessel noticed that one man sitting at the head table hadn't been introduced. The man was identified as George Trautman, president of the minor leagues, and he was introduced. There seemed to be no doubt left about where the minor leagues stood with the majors.

THE NEARNESS OF DEATH

(August, 1959)

(This had been a harrowing night. The College All-Stars had played so poorly, the game had been so dull. No one really understood what had happened until the players came out of the dressing room with their story of fright on the field.

There has never been a boy with more confidence than Lee Grosscup. Here, though, he revealed himself as still a boy with the fears of a boy, the kind whose head you want to pat and send home to his pajamas.

The night must have had a lasting impact on him, for at this writing, Grosscup still had not become a playing member of the New York Giants, who drafted him.)

CHICAGO—The vice president of the United States, Richard M. Nixon, had visited the steamy clamminess of the College All-Stars dressing room like the swarm of working journalists, consoled the dispirited disciples of the campus pastime in defeat and taken his leave.

In this gesture he played a professed frustration to the limit of its convenience, for at the annual meeting of the Football Writers of America he had revealed that he was actually a sidetracked sports writer caught up by the overwhelming urge of politics.

The Collegians, 29–0 victims of the Baltimore Colts Friday evening, returned to their bodily attentions and soon they were dressed and slipping out into the night after saying quiet goodbyes to teammates who had become close friends.

One of these, Lee Grosscup, a quarterback from the University of Utah, walked down the ramp under Soldier Field's east side wearing loafers, dark trousers, a conservative sports jacket and a somewhat vacant stare. That night he had been delegated by Coach Otto Graham to start the game and he had received his professional baptism under heavy fire.

On Saturday he would fly to Hershey, Pennsylvania, where he would join the New York Giants, who had drafted and signed him to a no-cut contract. His face was a shaken countenance, as a weary warrior returned from the blood and the hell of trench combat. It is a bright face, clean, handsome and a bit fine for the gore and the grime of football's clash of flesh.

"It wouldn't have been as bad if . . . well, it was all different after Don Brown got hurt," he said. "He was dead, I mean dead, and we all saw him lying there on the ground."

On the second play of the All-Stars' second offensive series, Grosscup had sent Brown, a 195-pound halfback from the University of Houston, flaring out on a pass play. In full flight Brown had run into the elbow of Bill Pellington, a 230-pound Baltimore linebacker, and he came down like a felled post.

"He lay there kicking," Grosscup said, "and I just thought he had been shaken up a little bit, but then he began to turn blue in the face. The people came on the field to look at him, then all of a sudden everybody began dashing around like mad.

"Somebody, Gino Marchetti, I think, saw what had happened. Don had swallowed his tongue and was choking to death. The doctor from the Baltimore bench got down and gave him mouth-to-mouth respiration and he was purple by that time.

"I turned away then. I couldn't watch any longer. He was dead. He'd quit breathing. I couldn't believe it. I'd gone to the movie with him the night before. We'd become good friends. I think if he'd have died I'd have walked off that field and never played another game of football. That really shook us up, just took the starch right out of us."

Brown was revived, taken to a hospital and Saturday was returned to good health, but Lee Grosscup reflected the morale-withering impact of his injury. Two plays afterward the All-Star center snapped the ball over the punter's head for a safety. Within six minutes two Baltimore touchdowns hurriedly developed and an early decision was reached in the twenty-sixth game of a mid-summer sporting tradition.

Once in the second half, while Weeb Ewbank played a mixture of Colts new and old, the Collegians did carry an offensive to the three-yard line. But the drive had the tepid character of the "whisper offense" of the Chicago White Sox— a base on balls, a stolen base, an infield out and score on a sacrifice fly.

Three times this All-Stars offensive was revived by penalties, once by pass interference and once by the recovery of a fumbled punt.

While the Colts were enthusiastically setting a new record for penalties, the All-Stars were setting a new record for cleanliness. As if doing their good deed for the day, they had become the first college team that ever played the pros without losing a foot to the officials.

It appeared they might have been too clean and upright for their own good. The Colts, understand, had not been abusive and underhanded. They had simply been aggressive and direct.

The fact is, some of the Baltimore coaches were rather provoked at the officials, and there were suggestions that one of them might win the most-valuable award, for they had gained much more ground than the college runners.

George Strickler, a Chicago *Tribune* observer of football since the Four Horsemen were foals, appeared to have wrapped up the package rather compactly with the lead paragraph of his story of the game.

"The men from Baltimore played the boys from college last night," George wrote. "The boys lost."

This enthusiasm for the Colts' maturity was not shared wholly by Coach Ewbank, who had seen them postpone capture of the National Football League championship last season until the sudden death appendage of the play-off game.

"A good start on the season, huh?" Ewbank was asked.

"Maybe," said he, through pursed lips, "but I'm glad we weren't playing the New York Giants tonight." Indicating that it might have been sudden death of another nature.

THE LAST 'BIG THURSDAY'

(October, 1959)

(*For years the "Big Thursday" state fair football game between South Carolina and Clemson was one of the major sports rituals in the South. There wouldn't be another. Lobbying and legislation had taken care of that. Clemson people were tired of playing such a vital game as this on the road every year, and while you couldn't blame them, you surely couldn't blame yourself for shedding a few tears over the passing of such a lovely tradition.*

It was a Roman holiday, a festival, a wild caper on the village green. I had seen roosters' necks wrung, gates stampeded, fist fights fought by gentlemen in dress suits, and drunks toted out like sacks of fertilizer. This didn't make it a classic, but it did give the occasion some sporting body and flavor.)

★ ★

COLUMBIA, S.C.—As streaks of eastern light cracked the skies of South Carolina this Thursday morning, many a Sandlapper arose from his bed and dressed in his garish best while in the kitchen his bride packed the picnic basket. Flasks were filled with tonic water, in case venomous snakes were encountered on this hazardous journey, and shortly they set out, hardy pioneers advancing on the state capital.

From Wampee to Walhalla, from Yemassee to Tamassee this little drama of the dawn was enacted. Fathers, mothers, daughters and sons, alumni, alumnae and spiritual affiliates, politicians, storekeepers and bankers, doctors, lawyers, bakers and thieves, alcoholics, teetotalers, preachers and bartenders all were going the same way.

There was a funeral of an old friend to attend.

This is a strange way to prepare for a funeral, but this is a strange old friend. Precisely at 2 P.M. in Carolina Stadium, a steel saucer located on the state fair grounds in Columbia, last rites would begin for Big Thursday.

This is the last of the great series between South Carolina and Clemson that began in 1896 and had reached such a degree of bigness as to become a national classic in itself. This is because it is the only college football game played in America on this day, and because it therefore enjoys the undivided attention of the nation.

This had become too much for Clemson College. Each year the Tigers had to play their most important game on the soil of their most vicious rival. Win or lose, whatever came afterward was a letdown for one or the other. It might be said, however, that Clemson did make the most remarkable resurgence of any Big Thursday victim last year.

Slaughtered 26–6 at the State Fair, the Tigers moved on to the championship of the Atlantic Coast Conference and played to millions in the Sugar Bowl.

Nevertheless, the game had become so big that Clemson, its highest authorities, its coach and athletic director, Frank Howard, its alumni and its students had reached a common agreement.

South Carolina should be met on Clemson soil at least once every other year. Negotiations began. Fire flew. Old-liners didn't like the idea. Gamecocks didn't like the idea. Downstate Clemson alumni didn't like the idea. But Clemson liked the idea, and since Clemson owned one of the football teams appearing, and since Clemson was able to muster enough support in the state legislature, Clemson swung things Clemson's way.

Big Thursday was declared dead. The Clemson-South Carolina game was moved to the last Saturday of November, to be played alternately in Carolina Stadium, seating 42,000, and Clemson Stadium, seating 40,000 and equipped with an elevator to the press box.

This day will be no different from any of the rest, except that it will be the last of the Big Thursdays. These Sandlappers will come and they will whoop and they will holler. There will not be enough tickets for all who'd like to see it. Some will get too drunk and have to be toted home. Some will sing and celebrate until their heads split.

Because this is the kind of day it is, and because it enjoys national exclusiveness, whatever has happened here has been magnified. Two events, however, would have forced attention on most any occasion, for they shall never be forgotten.

There was the year the former baseball umpire and associates forged about 10,000 tickets and distributed them about the state. A few minutes before the kickoff a wild commotion arose at the stadium gates. People with legitimate tickets were being turned away, and people with bogus tickets were demanding admittance.

The thwarted ones vowed to get in somehow, and somehow they did.

There were two huge wooden gates at one end of the stadium, and the angry ticketholders amassed at this entrance. Together they pushed and shoved until about midway of the first quarter the gates came crashing down, and 5,000 to 10,000 human beings surged into Carolina Stadium.

There weren't enough police in South Carolina to restore order, and so the human cattle milled about the place until the surface of the football field was the only patch of earth left exposed.

Gregarious fans intermingled with players and coaches. Generously some of them offered players drinks from their flasks.

One man sidled up to Rex Enright, then the Carolina coach, and said, "Why don't you put ol' 67 in, Coach? He's from my hometown and they's a crowd of us up here'd like to see him play."

That was in '46. It was a year later, I think, that some Clemson gallant rushed out onto the field, captured Carolina's gamecock mascot and ran up and down the field wringing the poor fowl's neck.

This almost started a war. Not only were Carolinians irate, but the Society for Prevention of Cruelty to Animals rose up in protest. Clemson is said to have punished the game student, but I've always suspected that as soon as he returned to the old campus he was extolled as the autumn hero.

In '48, the only perfect team in the history of the two schools used this game as a springboard, but it wasn't at all easy. Clemson won in the last few minutes on a blocked punt by Phil Prince and a touchdown recovery by Oscar Thompson, a runty little end from Columbia.

Carolina had led almost from the start, when Bo Hagan, now backfield coach at Rice, threw a scoring pass to Red Wilson of Macon and Bayard Pickett kicked the extra point. Clemson scored, but missed the extra point, and then the game was in the dying stages, Carolina punting to protect its lead when the punt was blocked and suddenly it was Clemson's day.

Big Thursday isn't exactly dead in South Carolina. It merely moves to November and becomes Big Saturday. But for the rest of the nation, the other forty-nine states which have shared the high moments of this Roman holiday in October, it dies at sundown, or when the last drop is downed, and when the last weary body has been returned to its bed back in Wampee, Walhalla, Yemassee or Tamassee.

NORTH VERNON, IND., ON A
SUNDAY AFTERNOON

(June, 1958)

(I had to see what North Vernon was like the day after Pat O'Connor was killed at Indianapolis. The little town drew me like a magnet. I stopped at a filling station and got some gas, and the attendant said it sure was a shame.

I drove by the church, and by his motel, and by the cemetery where they were to bury him. I thought of the injustice of it, for O'Connor was the finest, most admirable young man I ever met among the fast racing set.

As an ironical conclusion to the story, Ed Elisian, whose "charging" down the backstretch set off the crash, was later broiled to death in a mishap at Milwaukee, and Jimmy Reece, whose nervous foot compounded the calamity, later was the guest of honor at one of these 2 P.M. church services, killed on a track in the East.)

NORTH VERNON, Ind.—North Vernon is a shady little county seat town in southeast Indiana, between Indianapolis and Madison. Sunday morning the people were dressing and leaving the house for church like usual. Sunday afternoon they went back to church again, but this time it wasn't like usual.

This time they all went to the First Baptist Church, as many as could get in. They went to say their goodbys to Pat O'Connor, the clean young man who had graduated from high school into racing cars, and who had died Friday sitting erect in his burning racer on the northeast turn at Indianapolis.

Race drivers, as a breed, are gypsies. After they surrender to the urge of speed, home is where they drove their last race, or where they're scheduled to drive their next one. But home to Pat O'Connor was North Vernon.

He always went back there. This was his anchor.

South of town Pat O'Connor's Motel, a simple little tourist village in a grove of shade trees, was closed. A funeral wreath hung on the office door. Another wreath hung on the door of the Greenleaf Grill, which is a part of the court. Still another wreath hung on the door of Pat O'Connor's Laundromat, adjacent to the motel.

These were O'Connor's investments, further testimony to his nativity, to his belief in his future in North Vernon. But first, before he settled down to it all, he wanted to make one appearance in Victory Lane at Indianapolis. Something told him to. That urge that race drivers get. It would mean something to him to be remembered as a man who had won the toughest race in the world. Besides, then he could afford improvements on his motel. Really make it something.

One thing about it, when the pastor stood up to say his last words over Pat O'Connor, he wouldn't have to make any apologies for him. Everybody in town was proud of him. He was everything that handsome, boyish face said he was. And you thought of the way it happened and it made you sick.

The vastness of Indianapolis Speedway is a thing hard to envision unless you're there. It's so large, for instance, that the nine-hole golf course contained in the infield covers no more area than a biscuit in your hand. There's still room enough to park 40,000 cars, accommodate 75,000 people, maintain a hospital and fifty-four garages and preserve in its original beauty a little creek.

So, when a crash occurs, it may be out of sight. The first reaction is the flashing of the yellow caution light, and then the starter, Bill Vandewater, will jump onto the track waving the yellow flag. Sometimes it's thirty minutes or more before you find out what has happened.

The helpless pit crews can only stand and watch the cars go past and hope they spot their own. That's how they know they're still in business.

That's how it was on Memorial Day. The Sumar Special crew didn't see O'Connor's car come back around. Several others didn't make it either, but O'Connor's crew set out in a trot across the big infield.

Nobody said much in the press box. Some of the drivers coming in had said, "It's really a mess back there." Several seats down the press row somebody was heard to say, "It's verified. O'Connor's dead." A wire service man was rushing out the news, but nobody went to find out. You didn't want to know.

Of course the detonator was the Ed Elisian-Dick Rathmann collision. They were having a bout of their own, and most of the rest of the worst of it would have been avoided. But what set off the chain reaction that led to death was a braking car.

Jimmy Reece, in No. 16, had gone to the brakes. His was the third car. Everybody behind him had to scatter looking for a way around him. Bob Veith, to the left of O'Connor, bounced off Reece, but found running room and got by.

O'Connor hurdled Reece and skidded upside down and that was the end of it. This is a weird sport. In other games you make a mistake and it costs you two free throws, or a fifteen-yard penalty, or a ten-day suspension, or a $25 fine.

In this game, it costs you your life. It may not be your mistake, but you still pay.

Death is always present, but seldom ever given the courtesy of acknowledgement. They speak in terms of caution and care and warning, but they never say for what. They never say it's for the privilege of living another day.

They were showing a film at the Speedway last week, taken by a camera mounted over Jimmy Bryan's left shoulder as he drove an exhibition run at 140–150 m.p.h. The film would take your breath away. Even veterans of the track were surprised at the sensation.

Two drivers, Reece and Troy Ruttman, rushed out to fetch the owners of their cars. "I want him to see what it's like," Reece said. "Maybe he'll raise my cut."

But raise or no raise, Reece races on firmly convinced that nobody will ever have to go to services for him at 2 P.M. on a sunny Sunday afternoon.

THE 'LUCKY AMATEUR'

(June, 1960)

(This was the milling scene at the worst-conducted promotion I have ever covered in sports, the second world heavyweight title fight between Floyd Patterson and Ingemar Johansson. Our doting Americans, quick to idolize anything imported, had created a great myth about the Swede. He had a ring through the nose of some of our finest sports writers and authorities, and they had begun to believe him invincible.

He went down early and stayed out a long time, long enough to miss the agony of the scramble at ringside, where the press corps was left unattended to fend off New York maniacs and other unlicensed invaders as best they could.

But the most astonishing note of the evening from my standpoint was the verdict delivered by the two Swedish sports writers who sat next to me, which is the meat of this column.

I might add that since I had picked Patterson by a knockout, I found no cause to quarrel with their verdict or the outcome.)

NEW YORK—This is a sight not to be forgotten for a long while. Floyd Patterson directed his left hand to the chin of Ingemar Johansson in the fifth round and the Swedish heavyweight was sent sprawling to the canvas Monday night at the Polo Grounds.

As Johansson lay there, a sort of sneer spread over Patterson's face.

A moment later Patterson again put a left in Johansson's

face. This time the dying swan of Goteborg went down with a dull thud. Patterson, meanwhile, walked to a neutral corner, turned his back on the scene, and leaned casually across the ropes on his elbows in the position of a man about to order a beer.

This was the end of it. Johansson had been knocked into a state of total humility. Patterson, in 13 minutes and 51 seconds of fighting time, had won vindication, had rewon the world's heavyweight title of boxing, and had taken the confident Swedish champion of free love down a peg or two, as they say in provincial circles.

The devastation of Johansson was so complete that it is now necessary to direct your attention to his dressing room, in the center-field section of the Polo Grounds.

It was no easy trip. Pandemonium had broken out in the old arena up in Harlem. Enthusiastic supporters of Patterson had burst through police and were scrambling to get in the ring with him. The peons and the lackeys of Feature Sports, Inc., had taken no advance measures to prevent such bedlam.

People were crushed. Birgit Lundgren, Johansson's close female friend, tried to get to the ring and the side of her lover, who was stretched out in a deep sleep while trainers and doctors worked over him, but was turned back.

There was only one way to describe it. The Polo Grounds Monday evening was one helluva mess.

Now in the dressing room that once was the bath house of the New York Giants, Johansson was concealed behind a curtain. No outsiders were welcome.

Mother Johansson, father, sister, brother and Birgit joined him. After the longest wait, Edvin Ahlquist, who is referred to as Johansson's "adviser," came out to speak for his client. He was indeed solemn.

"He is all right," Ahlquist said in Swedish-American. "Is no talk. He would like to talk to the press tomorrow. He does not feel like talk tonight.

"I am sure this is understood. He is shocked. It is the first time in his life he has been knocked out and it is a terrible thing for him."

"Patterson got knocked out last year and he talked to the press," said a very strong pair of lungs across the room.

"This is his wish," Ahlquist said, as if speaking for a body laid out in the next room.

"The best man won. There are no alibis," and on into the virtues of a bout just witnessed.

In a moment a publicity man came out and reported that mother was crying, sister was crying, father was crying and Ingemar was in a daze. There was no report on the emotions of Birgit.

There could have been no happier place on earth than the dressing room of Patterson. The restored champion was overwhelmed by any number of gate-crashers who elbowed past dilatory cops into his dressing room.

Outside his door, Negroes jammed against each other screaming for a view of him, now recommissioned their hero. There was to be little sleep in Harlem Monday night. Everybody had to celebrate. "No, he didn't hurt me much," Patterson said to somebody who had asked him about the Johansson right that got to his jaw in the second round. "I was trying to get him to come to me and this did it."

This was the critical moment. This was the blow that won the fight and it didn't knock down anybody.

Patterson had stood up under Johansson's frightful right. The weapon that Johansson himself had come to speak of in reverent tones had been returned to mythology.

The Johansson right is now nothing more than the hand with which he feeds himself and brushes his teeth and signs checks.

Patterson, thus reassured and confident, took it from there and finished off his man in brutal fashion. In the first round, when Patterson had reddened Johansson's dimpled face with a series of stinging jabs followed up by some stiff rights of his own, the Swede had shown definite signs of distress.

He did not appear to like it inside the ring at all. He appeared flustered and hurt. In the third round Patterson went for the body and Johansson was punished. In the fourth round Johansson was in constant retreat and the times he did attempt to get a message through to that mystic right of his, the hand pawed around like the limb of a playful animal.

In the fifth came the end of the fantasy of the year. When Prince Ingemar woke up, he found he had been returned to the human race. He found a lump under his left eye and another one in his throat.

Cus D'Amato, Patterson's manager, was on his way into the ring, waving his black homburg above his head and shouting in triumph. This time Napoleon had won at Waterloo.

There had been two sports writers from Sweden sitting next to me, and this had happened in the hour before the two gladiators appeared in the ghastly glare of the ring lights..

"How is Johansson regarded in Sweden?" I had asked Nils Lofstrand of a Stockholm paper.

"I think," said Nils Lofstrand, surprisingly candid, "that he is a lucky amateur who has great strength but is not a good boxer. He is a lucky amateur who got over one strong punch, and my comrade agrees with me."

On this occasion Johansson was a clumsy uncoordinated fellow with no devastation in his famous right, a pretty fellow whose face betrayed an inner desire to turn and run. He was a shameful defender of the heavyweight championship of the world. Patterson had exposed him for what he is.

HOLLYWOOD WOULD NEVER BUY THIS

(October, 1960)

(Bobby Dodd Sr., the football coach, would not allow Bobby Dodd Jr. to come to Georgia Tech and play football for him. It was a loaded situation of which he wanted no part. Too, he wanted young Bobby to get a fair chance, which he felt he would not get in the abnormal circumstance of father coaching quarterback son.

Young Bobby went to Florida instead, fully scholarshipped. Ray Graves, Dodd's first assistant at Georgia Tech and closest friend for many years, went to Florida soon afterward as head coach.

On this dramatic Saturday afternoon in Gainesville, Florida, they all met again in one big collision of family, heart and sentiment. I've never watched a football game with a feeling quite like this, concerned as much as anything else with the mental and spiritual torment that was gnawing at the wife and the mother of these two Bobbys. Alice Dodd took it like a pioneer woman. I admired her, I believe, as much as either of the menfolk involved.

And the ending—well, it was simply too unreal for anyone ever to attempt in fiction.)

★ ★

GAINESVILLE, Fla.—Mounting the stadium steps at Florida Field in Gainesville Saturday came a broad, bulky man. When he reached a row high in the stands, about the thirty-seven-yard line, he turned off and sat down in seat No. 15.

He wore a broad smile on his face and warmly greeted several people sitting in his neighborhood. It may have been a mask of congeniality he was wearing, but it appeared to be real.

Then he sat down and waited for the show to start, and when it did, he was entertained by two hours and twenty minutes of the gol-darndest crop of football he'll ever see.

University of Florida defeated Georgia Tech 18–17, and in the course of it, George Robert Woodruff, holder of seat No. 15, high up on the thirty-seven-yard line, saw what they had wanted of him at Florida, why he was discarded as the head coach and replaced by Ray Graves.

Wild, daring, gambling, reckless, frenzied, sometimes foolish football took place.

I have a feeling that it wouldn't have made a great lot of difference to the Gator Growlers if quarterback Larry Libertore and fullback Jon MacBeth had missed on the two-point conversion that won the game with thirty-two seconds left. It was assuring enough that they'd gone for it.

It was the signature of a new regime, a regime that would gamble. It may have been the beginning of a new era in football at Florida.

The finish was utterly absurd. No self-respecting movie firm would look twice at such a manuscript, the coach's sophomore son helping his father's former chief assistant beat his father in the dying moments of the son's first big game on his own campus. Too obvious.

The Dodd angle, Bobby Sr. and Bobby Jr., had been whipped to a froth in the buildup. Next to nothing was expected to come of it, really.

That the outcome should linger in doubt until such a point, and that young Dodd should figure so prominently in the resolving of the issue in such a snake-pit of seething emotion was simply carrying the thing too far.

There's no removing Libertore from his pedestal. He was the climactic force. But it was Dodd Jr. who bodily lifted the ox out of the ditch on the drive to the touchdown that won. The Gators had been thrown back to their forty-two-yard line. The down was third with nineteen yards to go.

Dodd Jr. was rushed aboard with a play. He dropped straight

back and lofted a pass that halfback Don Deal caught at Tech's twenty-five for a thirty-three-yard gain.

There was to be no retreat for the Gators now. They had the emotional impetus and they moved on in, but not without the aid of Dodd Jr. again. He ran a quarterback sneak for a first down at the three, then recovered a fumble at the very door to the end zone, saving it all.

It was an exhilarating triumph for him, and he went off to his Saturday night date in good humor. His father maintained a stout front at all times, but the defeat cut him deeply. This was twice within a year he had been defeated by a former assistant, in the Gator Bowl by Frank Broyles, and now by Graves, abetted by his own son.

For Alice Dodd, wife and mother, it was even worse. Besieged by magazine photographers throughout the day, eavesdropped upon by snooping reporters who infiltrated the stands around her and stared at her like a curiosity, she was ripped to emotional shreds. It's almost inhuman to put a woman through such an ordeal.

The Georgia Tech team could have saved Mrs. Dodd a good deal of grief. The Jackets played the first quarter as if in a trance. They were sluggish. They moved lead-footedly downfield on punts and kickoffs, until they found they were in for a furious fight.

They never really got with it in the manner of which they seem capable. But perhaps they were only suffering by comparison beside the dedicated Gators, who attacked in the suicidal manner of a wave of Japanese banzai troops. They, the Gators, subsisted on effort and determination beyond human limitations.

Yet, they were never ahead until the last thirty-two seconds. Let this be said for them, though. In this frenetic moment of football, when all strategy and tactic seemed more the product of happenstance than plan, they never strayed so far from the realm of reason as to lose sight of the most desirable stage at which to be in front.

Some Emotion, Some Sentiment and Some Crisis

WHERE THE TAXI CABS ROAM, ETC.

(August, 1957)

(Ken Loeffler, the basketball coach, and I had had breakfast one morning during the previous winter. He had spoken candidly of his failure to warm up to Texas, and vice versa. I had written a column on his observations, which were not at all in line with what they observe at Texas A&M.

He had been fired, or forced to resign. In the meantime, both he and his former boss, Paul (Bear) Bryant, athletic director at Texas A&M, had been booked to appear as lecturers at a clinic in Atlanta.

Both had just reached town. The atmosphere was thick enough to cut with a bread knife. Bryant and Loeffler hadn't seen each other since the firing. Loeffler, meanwhile, had promised to blow the lid off a scandal at A&M. He talked an enraged game. It seemed wise to frisk him. When they met, though, Bryant and Loeffler were disappointingly cordial. Not a blow was struck or a shot fired.)

★ ★

Dwight Keith is a quiet man with no desire for controversy or any affiliation with the International Boxing Club. But he does have a flair for matchmaking that surely would save the prize fight industry a reservation for oblivion. He is the man responsible for sport's Coincidence of the Year.

Keith is the booking agent for the Georgia Athletic Coaches Association Clinic. It was absolutely coincidental that he should have booked at the same clinic this week Ken Loeffler, formerly of Texas A&M, and Bear Bryant, still of Texas A&M.

These men are not friends. It is quite possible, however, that they do have great respect for one another. At any rate, they will be housed under the same Biltmore Hotel roof for one evening, beginning with Bryant's arrival Tuesday, bringing them closer together than they have been since "it" happened.

Several weeks ago Texas A&M was excused from the probation list of the NCAA. It was another coincidence that just before this Loeffler had resigned as basketball coach at A&M and it seems that A&M got off because Loeffler got out.

Confronted with this incriminating line of reasoning in the dimness of a Biltmore lounge, Loeffler nodded his learned head and agreed that sure enough, this is the way it must have looked.

"But," he said, and he is an eloquent fellow, "by the intelligent searcher of knowledge and truth, and by those who have been exposed to the many angles of this situation, it is known that I took a rap.

"I could have stayed on and fought it out. But I have a wife and a small boy to consider. I have friends at Texas A&M who would have been caught in the fire. And why should I defend a situation I had no desire to hold? I have never been so happy to leave a state as I was to leave the state of Texas."

Play no chorus of "Home on the Range" (". . . where the buffalo roam and the sky is not cloudy all day," etc.) for this man. Give him a home where taxi cabs roam, and a man's corral is an apartment eight floors up and the sky is sometimes smoggy and gray.

This he has again. He is back now in Philadelphia, and when the college season begins, he will be on the staff at Monmouth College in Asbury Park, New Jersey. He will be assistant to the president, a public relations man at work on television and the speaker's rostrum. In time he will return to coaching. He has no alternative. His very nature will allow nothing else.

In the beginning, all was meant for love between Bryant and Loeffler. Each is a distinct individualist. Together they might have conquered Texas and had the whole immature state for their private oyster.

But within two weeks after Loeffler had transferred from La Salle College in Philadelphia to College Station, A&M was pitched on the probation list because of football sin. From this seed, the antagonism grew.

Football had to be king. Bryant had left the shadow of Adolph Rupp in Kentucky to escape this pressure of the bouncing ball. And for an income of $40,000 a year—$15,000 salary, $10,000 from two concerns as member of the board, and a $5,000 television commitment.

The actual story can't be told, for Loeffler reserves this for future magazine business. His testimony, however, indicates that an alumnus in Houston presented a basketball player from the East his fare home for Christmas. A&M was convicted on the charge and Loeffler was charged with the crime and the yeast began to act.

"Chicken feed," he said, stormily. "That was merely chicken feed. They had to have something to make it look as if they were cleaning up down there. Football had to be king. Basketball had to take the rap.

"If they really want something to put the blast on the Aggies, they should look under the football table. It would sicken the strongest stomach."

Strangely, Loeffler feels no strong enmity for Bryant. "I have only respect for a man who sees what he wants and drives for it the way Bryant does," he said. "Survival of the fittest—that's the basis of our civilization. If he walked in here now, he would say, 'Ken, I wanted to help you. But you were talking when you should have been listening.' That's what he'd say. And he'd put his arm around me. You've got to admire a big, strong, impressive fellow like that."

The crowning blow to A&M came in a column from Atlanta last December, while the Aggie basketball team was here for a game at Georgia Tech. "College Station is a great place for old ladies and children," Loeffler had said, "but I don't think the old man can last."

"That did it," Loeffler said now. "When I got back to Texas

they were waiting for me. You know, if you'd only written that I laughed or smiled when I said it, that would have made it all right. In Texas, I've found out, they're awfully sensitive about Texas."

THE HOLDOUT

(February, 1957)

(*No event is quite so overrated in news value as the news that some baseball player has inked a pact, as they say on the sports pages. Of course he has inked a pact. He prefers to eat rather than starve through the summer months.*

On occasion, though, there will be some hardy bargaining before the pact-inking. Some player-fellow will put up a strenuous howl about the financial injustice being done his talent. This can develop into a test of two supremely stubborn dispositions and, after a period of time has passed, the stubborn player will become a holdout.

I had arrived early for spring training this year in order to firm up, as they say on Madison Avenue, a magazine story with Warren Spahn about how Milwaukee would win the world championship. Bob Buhl and John Quinn were in the painful throes of negotiations, and holdout Buhl was putting up a stiff fight.

P. S.: Buhl signed the next day for a $5,000 raise. Milwaukee did win the pennant and the World Series, and everybody was happy ever after, or for a reasonable length of time, at least.)

★ ★

BRADENTON, Fla.—From the broad porch of the Milwaukee clubhouse you could sit and watch a fellow holding out. It was not a strenuous process, but it was something rare to the naked eye.

Just that morning Gene Conley had signed. The tall pitcher and General Manager John Quinn of the Braves had stood out in foul territory near the left-field fence and negotiated. In no time they agreed on terms.

A little while later, Quinn and Bob Buhl took their stances in the same region. This was a resumption of hostilities. One day last week they had stood in the same spot three hours and hemmed and hawed and bargained and haggled.

Once again time dragged on and the twosome stood firm. It appeared they were going for the record of three hours. Occasionally they were at close quarters. Then they'd draw apart. Buhl would paw the earth with the toe of his crepe-soled shoes, as he would paw the mound in County Stadium.

Holding out, while not physically exerting, obviously was mentally taxing. Two hours and forty-five minutes later they broke it up still in disagreement, too exhausted to improve on their first performance. This would require one of Quinn's neatest jobs of negotiation.

Conley offered a fairly simple problem. He had won only eight games and been disappointing. Buhl had won eighteen, his best record. A couple of seasons ago, though, Buhl had suffered a blight that seriously damaged his earning power. He has not yet recovered from that barren summer.

Buhl walked into the clubhouse and some of the Braves asked him if he'd signed yet. He shook his head with a scowl.

The battery men were in from some work under the gently baking Florida sun. They were still moist with their first sweat of spring training. Already some had blisters on their feet and an early bird or two had sore legs.

"Are you close together?" one of them asked Buhl.

"Not nearly as close as I think we ought to be," he said. "About all I can say is that we're a little closer together than when we started."

Buhl sat down on a trunk and flopped against the wall. He pulled out a knife and started scraping flakes of paint off the equipment trunk.

"I'm not anxious," he said. "I can pass up all this work, anyway. I'm in good shape. I'll give it a couple more days, and if nothing happens I'll probably drive my wife and kids to Wisconsin—they been down here six weeks—and fly back. I don't need all this work, anyway."

Buhl chipped some more paint and it was quiet except for the plop-plop of the rubber sandals of Braves walking by on their way to the showers. A photographer came up, shoved a paper in Buhl's hands and took his picture. The holdout's expression never changed, except he may have looked just a little sheepish.

The photographer thanked him and left. Buhl chipped some more paint.

For a short while the holdout lost the stage in the clubhouse to the first misquote of the season. A Milwaukee newspaperman had written that Manager Fred Haney would fine any Brave $500 who strays out of line this season. None of the other newspapermen who'd been there at the time remembered such a financial threat.

"I don't have any do's or don'ts for this team, in spite of Jackie Robinson," he'd said. "They know what they're here for. Later on we may have some. Right now we haven't."

This was significant, especially in view of Robinson's banquet table potshot last month at the runners-up. The public, in other words, wants to know if Haney or the Braves were moved by what appears to have been idle gossip.

"I paid no attention to it," Haney said. "On the other hand, I'd be willing to wager you that nobody felt worse about it the next day than Robinson himself."

But that was another day and another crisis. Back in the clubhouse, Buhl was going out the door with Quinn again. The porch was vacant now, except for an elderly man in a floppy-brimmed hat down at the other end. Buhl and Quinn sat down and talked quietly, firmly but calmly, and they shook their heads.

The fellow in the floppy-brimmed hat kept trying to light his pipe in the wind. His name: Edd Roush, once a National League outfielder and its leading hitter.

In 1930 Roush staged one of the stubbornest holdouts of all time. He refused what the Giants offered and sat out the entire season. He never cared for spring training, anyway.

Now, he lives in Bradenton and seldom misses a practice.

(There is no more nervous player of golf than Dr. Cary Middlecoff. I walked into the lower clubhouse at Augusta that afternoon in time to watch him in the throes of mental contortions before he set out upon the course to defend the lead he held.

It was good for him to have Jack Burke around, for Jack, also kind of nervous, provided a good buffer between Middlecoff and the screaming meemies.

It was an excruciatingly beautiful view of two great professional golfers and their worries and frets before pulling on their uniforms of pressurized aloneness in which they play their tournament game. You'll note that they talk about everything, frequently light-hearted, frequently serious, but always coming back to their mental burden.

It all worked out fine for the Memphis dentist. He shot a 70 that day and held his lead and won a green coat, signifying a Masters victory, with a total of 279.)

AUGUSTA—Cary Middlecoff, DDS, walked into the stillness of the lower clubhouse at Augusta National and recklessly threw his long chassis at a nubby green couch. He had eaten a hearty breakfast of orange juice and scrambled eggs. He would eat no lunch, for he was scheduled to resume his attack on the Masters at 1:42. He would take his hay fever pill. He would have a few minutes reserved for a final visit to the putting green.

"Can anybody give me a decent idea of the time?" he said.

"One minute past one," said a loiterer.

Jack Burke was there. He'd shod himself and now he pulled on several gloves, suggesting as he did that the manufacturer who'd made the things should have to wear them.

"You have to buy a dozen pair to get one to fit," he groused.

"I'd be lying," Middlecoff said, "if I didn't admit that I'm a little jumpy. But I'd rather be where I am than to be four strokes out."

"I'm just sitting here trying to figure out where I can pick up five strokes," Burke said. "I've got to gamble. You get a 72 or a 73 and you're in."

"I'd like to have a 72," Middlecoff said. "I'd like to come in with my par."

"I got the idea you were having your toughest fight with yourself yesterday about the fourth and fifth holes," the loiterer said. "You were looking at your putts a little longer. On the fourth you made five trips back and forth looking over a little three-footer."

"I was no more nervous there than anywhere else. I wasn't the carefree-est guy on the course any time. Even Eadie's got the jitters. She's worse than I am, I think. The first couple of years we were married she didn't show it much because she didn't know a driver from a sledge hammer. Then she learned more about it and she learned to work up a beautiful case of nerves."

He filled his cheeks full of air and exhaled with a rather soft phew.

"This is one where you play for the title, not the money," Burke said. "The others, you play for the money. This is a golf course. If you win this one they know when you're through that you can play a little golf."

"A good start means an awful lot here," Middlecoff said. "If you get past the first five or six holes, you can go the rest of the way. That good start's sure important, I tell you."

He jumped up and walked briskly to the closet. "I've got to take my hay fever pill. I've been lucky this year. That freeze was great for me. I know it's hurt the looks of the course, but I haven't been bothered at all."

"The paper says it's going to rain."

"Yeah? I didn't see that."

"That's what it said. 'Occasional rain in the afternoon.' That's the disadvantage about going off late. The wind's kicking up some now."

"I can't take that wind," Middlecoff said. "I'd almost as soon have rain."

"How much influence does the shot of a playing partner have on you, Cary? I'm thinking about the third hole yesterday, when you were short on your approach."

"Peter Thomson's shot cost me a stroke there. I saw him go over the green and I played mine too short. It really helps you, though, on the par threes. You know what club he's using and you're on the shot all the way.

"It almost cost me on the twelfth, watching Pete. He hit a six and overshot and I'm longer than he is. I started to hit my seven, then I decided I ought to use my six. Just as I hit it a puff of wind blew up and I wound up in the muck. I got down in three, but I had to put it to the pin."

"Golfers are like baseball players having hitting streaks, blowing hot and cold, and when you're hot you get the idea you can't miss anything."

"That's right," Middlecoff said. He was the winner at St. Petersburg and last Sunday tied the course record at North Fulton in Atlanta. "That 64 in Atlanta was mighty important to me. I'd used that new putting grip a couple of practice rounds over here. One was good and one was bad. I'd had the bad one the day before I played in Atlanta. Then I had that 64. I decided I liked that grip again. My putts have been dropping over here. That's why I've got those four strokes."

Burke said he'd talked to Jimmy Demaret down in Port Aransas, Texas, and that the missing pro had claimed that he'd caught all the fish in the Gulf of Mexico. Demaret missed the Masters this year for medical reasons.

"How about old Jim sitting down there fishing," Middlecoff said, "and we're sitting up here sweating? Man, they couldn't play a six-round tournament. Nobody would ever finish."

"Whatta you mean?" Burke asked.

"That tension. Nobody could stand that tension for six rounds.

"What time is it now?" he asked.

It was 1:20. "Well, I better go put in five minutes of consultation with my putter," Middlecoff said.

For one day, at least, all the nervous patients in the world got even with all their dentists. But by sundown the dentists had their customary edge again. Young Doc Middlecoff stood up there with the title that means more than money and where he'd been wearing all that tension he now wore one of those green coats of the champion.

A WATCH OVER THE RECKLESS

(May, 1961)

(These were trying days at Indianapolis, a little more so than normal in the last few hours before the Memorial Day 500-mile race. Tony Bettenhausen had been killed testing Paul Russo's car, and old "Cementhead" had been considered relatively indestructible.

He had flipped twenty-eight times in his racing career and had come back laughing. The twenty-ninth time he came back dying.

It was a personal tragedy to Lindsey Hopkins, the millionaire who owned the hot car that Bettenhausen was to have driven. It made him sick of racing, but he recovered in time and labored through the event half-heartedly.

Then there was this fellow Cliff Griffith, 45 years old and racing again after returning from the valley of death himself. It made you look at these fellows and wonder what on earth went on inside their physical factories.

P. S.: A. J. Foyt won and nobody got killed.)

INDIANAPOLIS, Ind.—It is rather difficult to be around Indianapolis these days without noticing that there is an automobile race in town on Tuesday. Airlines passengers disembark from their planes under archways that proclaim them "Welcome To The '500' Festival."

Filling stations, drug stores, beverage dispensaries, hardware stores, even funeral homes fly proudly the same banner, welcoming all potential clients to the area.

Once this was a carnival affair. Ferris wheels threshed the air around Indianapolis Speedway. Barkers shrilled out their lures to the suckers. Pinball machines, dice games, snake shows and other arts of an associated nature were practiced in every vacant lot near the track.

Once, not many seasons ago, midget racing prevailed on a quarter-mile track across 16th Street from the Speedway. The miniature cars spit their angry snarls out into the night from 9 P.M. to 3 A.M.

There were times when daring, and perhaps hungry Indianapolis drivers sneaked in a few racing licks in the midgets until Indianapolis authority closed down on this personel disregard for safety. Some of these fellows have to be protected from themselves.

This brought up the matter of Tony Bettenhausen, who died in the flames of Paul Russo's car at the Speedway on May 12. Without the intervention of death, Bettenhausen would be sitting in the cockpit of Lindsey Hopkins' Autolite Special Tuesday.

Instead, the pilot will be Lloyd Ruby of Houston, Texas, who finished seventh here last year in a J. C. Agajanian Special. Ruby suffered some differences with the Agajanian mechanic and there was a mutual disarrangement of contract.

"I asked Tony not to get in Russo's car," Lindsey said. "He begged me. I told him he was taking a useless chance. He begged me some more and I let him go.

"He took two laps over 146 (m.p.h.) and should have known all there was to know about the car. He slowed down like he was coming in, we waved him in, but he took off again.

"He wouldn't even look at us as he passed again. The next time around, all I saw was a flash. It was that magnesium wheel hitting the wall. Over he went and my driver was dead."

Some emotional scenes followed. For a day or two it seemed that Hopkins might close up his racing shop and quit. The shock wore off in time and he relented.

Then Russo, 47 years old and a grandfather, came to Hopkins

and said he would like to drive his No. 5 and win the race and give the money to Valerie, Mrs. Bettenhausen.

"This was just one of those emotional moments," Lindsey said. "I told him if he drove it, we'd keep it on a business basis.

"He took the car out and never got it above 144. It made me so nervous watching him. I knew we couldn't have that arrangement, and so I called it off."

Late in the afternoon of the day before the last qualifying weekend, Ruby blew the engine of his Kelso Special. He was out of a car. He was too good a driver to leave off the track.

The next day he took No. 5 out on the course and it was a lovely marriage of man and machine. "He was doing 146 and he'd never had any time in the car at all," Hopkins said, "and so I am pleased. The only thing is, he's pretty far back in the ninth row and that only gives him an opportunity to drive a lot."

All of this presents Hopkins a second leg on the frustration trophy.

In 1955 he came here with the machine and the driver. Bill Vukovich had won it two years in a row in other cars and chose the Hopkins Special to go for his third.

He was far out in front with only survival necessary when he ran into a sprawling, spinning series of collisions on the southeast turn at 150 miles per hour, went over the wall upside down and was roasted in his cockpit.

In 1953, a fellow from Ninevah, Indiana, named Cliff Griffith hit the southwest wall, leaped from his burning machine in spite of a broken pelvis and spent many months in Methodist Hospital under repair.

Now Griffith is 45 years old and a grandfather. He made a return to the Memorial Day field this year. He qualified at 145.03 m.p.h., which would have been positively frightening in his year of 1953. Today, it is plodding speed.

As Lindsey Hopkins left the hospital where Bettenhausen had been taken after his fatal run, one of the staff members stopped him at the desk.

"Tell that fellow Cliff Griffith," said the staff member, "to take his business to St. Joseph's this year. We don't want to go through that again."

Meaning, I suppose, that Cliff Griffith should know better. Some of them, as it is said, have to be protected from themselves.

Some of the Rare Species

A MOST WORTHY CHARITY

(November, 1959)

(You know the kind. You see them everywhere there is a baseball game, or a football game, or a boxing match, or a golf tournament, something that's major in the field. Each sport has its own "specialists."

Slim belonged to baseball. He was just as liable to pop up here or there as anywhere. He had no particular motive. He wanted to be a player, or a sports writer, and since he was neither, he was just doing his best to be attached.

He was a bother, but you had to admire his tenacity. He never allowed any rebuff to soften his approach. He was always there the next time. Nearly always he needed a bit of financial shoring-up, and nearly always he got it.

Maybe there was more method to Slim's system than I gave credit.)

Old Slim is the kind of fellow who can always be found loitering under the marquee or in the lobby of the hotel where baseball people are in congregation. Slim is better off than most such unanchored wanderers.

Most of them have only a thousand-mile shirt. Slim has both a thousand-mile shirt and a thousand-mile suit. It was once a sort of a gray suit, but it now is the color of Slim's hide, and around the seams a greenish trace of age is beginning to form.

The suit is apparently adaptable to all climates. Slim can be seen wearing it at spring training in Florida, at the major league

All-Star game in the heat of summer, and again at the World Series in autumn, when the nip is in the air.

He will be hanging around an entrance or an exit, and he will be carrying a 10x13 brown manila envelope, ragged and tattered from handling. The big envelope will be filled with faded clippings from sports sections, letters marked with grimy fingerprints addressed to Slim from important people, and other such timeless correspondence.

Most of the letters will say that the writer is sorry, but he can't oblige Slim, but that he (the writer) wishes Slim well. Then it will be signed, "Cordially, So-and-so."

And so Slim was sitting at the circular copy desk in the sports department when I walked in the other day. That handworn 10x13 brown envelope, fat with letters, clippings and other imperishable printed matter, lay on the desk before him.

Slim's hair was a little whiter. He ran his long, bony fingers through it as he sat and waited. The suit was a little seamier in spots, a little greener in others, but unquestionably bearing up remarkably in its supreme test.

Slim picked up his 10x13 and followed me into my corner office and stuck out his hand.

"I just want to tell you how my Old Troopers Memorial is coming along," Slim said. "It won't take but a few minutes."

He said that the profits realized from "The Greatest Show on Earth" had built seven hospitals, and that the funds from "Ten Commandments" were going to build several more. I asked him why he didn't use the money to buy a new suit and a shirt and get a haircut.

"What?" Slim said, appalled. "And use that money intended for a great charity for my own personal use?"

Of course the idea was utterly immoral. I just hadn't thought, that was all.

"Say," Slim said, "you know how I can get in touch with Luke Appling? Me and him are just like that."

Slim balled his bony hand into a bony fist.

"Here, let me show you this," Slim pulled out a ragged letter saying that Gov. Leroy Collins of Florida regretted it a great deal, but that he didn't feel that he could invite Luke Appling and Ted Lyons, "the two most popular heroes in the history of the Chicago White Sox," to be his guests at the World Series. The letter was signed by a secretary.

"See, I had it all lined up for Luke and Ted to go to the World Series," Slim said, "and they didn't show up."

I told Slim that I'd seen Luke at the World Series and that he appeared to be having a good time.

"That ol' sonofagun," Slim said, "and me up there looking for him all the time. You don't think ol' Luke was giving me the run-around, do you? And me and him just like that, ol' buddies."

Slim balled up his hand again.

"Now about the Old Troopers Memorial," I said. "I don't think I'm quite clear on that."

"Oh, you're a member," Slim said. "It's for guys in the trade like you. Here, did I ever show you this column that girl wrote about me in Sarasota?"

The print was almost worn off the ragged clipping, but it said a lot about Slim and his love for baseball. It didn't mention the Old Troopers Memorial.

"Oh, everybody in the trade across the country belongs," Slim said. "It's a great thing. We're raising funds every day, doing things for kids. Did I ever show you what I'm doing for kids all over the country?"

Slim fished around in the 10x13 envelope for a moment. Clippings about the sinking of the "Maine," the death of Floyd Collins, Babe Ruth's 700th home run and Peaches Browning fell out. He couldn't find the item about what he was doing for kids.

"I guess I musta misplaced it," Slim said. "That kills me, too, for I was getting a lot of things done to stop this juvenile stuff.

"By the way," he said, lowering his voice, "could you let me have a buck temporarily? I've come up short and I need a little loan to tide me over."

I fished out a buck, and I knew then what the dues were to

belong to the Old Troopers Memorial, of which I was now a full-fledged, paid-up member.

"You'll get it back at our next national meeting," Slim said, starting out the door. "I'll send you a report on all the things we're doing and the funds. We're trying to build seven more hospitals now, and if I can come up with just one more movie like 'The Greatest Show on Earth' . . ."

Slim just had to leave. He wanted to get off on another recruiting drive.

GEORGE W. SLEPT HERE

(August, 1960)

(*Every mother and every mother's son knows who Gorgeous George is. He is a creature of lovely confirmation with long, blond tresses and a manner that causes one to question his sexual intent.*

That famed old warhorse of wrestling, Ed (Strangler) Lewis, once said, "When he steps into the ring, I don't know whether to throw him or kiss him."

Gorgeous is a professional wrestler whose tale is fairly well covered here. He is as normal as wind in March and showers in May. He has only made a career of appearing questionable.

By this time, some of the gilt had worn off and Gorgeous was becoming slightly frayed around the edges. He was still a big draw, however, but he dwelled pleasurably only in the past. Tomorrow had seemed to become simply another awful awakening, infested with children, more alimony and another damned perfumed march to the ring.)

The first time Gorgeous George left his home in Houston, Texas to make his way in the cold, hard world, he came to Atlanta. He and another wrestler named Dizzy Davis shared a room in a small hotel that is now a flophouse. They paid $3.75 per week, double.

The George one, then not Gorgeous or famous, had been warned by his daddy, like all good fathers warned their sons in the days of Horatio Alger, that he would be home in six months, broke.

"I was broke several times, but I wasn't home in six months," Gorgeous George said the other day. "That's the last thing in the world I'd have done, gone home."

This was twenty-four years and several hundred tint jobs later. Gorgeous George had been back in Atlanta again for several days, flouncing about in rings well-sprayed by a new and modern advancement in wrestling, a female valet, or "valette." He has been paying the customers visits in the hustings as well as giving those admirers of his in Atlanta a well-rationed peek now and then.

On that first trip, he was 19 years old. He was also plain George Wagner, born on a farm in Boyd County, Nebraska, transferred to Texas by itinerant parents, and immediately prior to his indulgence in wrestling, a typewriter mechanic.

"I got into wrestling in self-defense," The Gorgeous One tells you. "We were having this pickup softball game one day and I got in an argument with the other team. I got so mad I said, 'I'll rassle all of you one at a time.'

"I did and I beat all seven of them. A man came along and watched me and he said he was a member of the YMCA and that he took his own little boy along sometimes. He said he'd like to take me. He took me and I started wrestling and that's the way it began."

A man named Hartung helped him with his wrestling lessons, and his beginning was without any of the pomp and splendor that accompanies the Gorgeous George performances today.

Somewhat nauseating as this is sometimes, it is beyond debating that this is the man whose presence and imagination has turned the business of professional wrestling inside out. Until he came along with his perfumes, his effeminate hair-stylings, his tailored velvet robes and his unmasculine affectations, wrestling was plodding along pretty well married to its old routines.

The wrestlers were sticking to muscle and grunting and groaning, and except for the flying tackle and the dropkick, introduced by two college men, Gus Sonnenberg of Dartmouth and Jumpin' Joe Savoldi of Notre Dame, there hadn't been much new in the catch-as-catch-can game in many years. There is still some doubt that what George Wagner introduced embodies progress, but it has created an interest that produced money and spectators for wrestling.

After George, there came a string of impersonators, or gimmick men. Gene Stanlee, "Mr. America," and Buddy Rogers, "Nature Boy," both grew long hair and dyed it blond and developed majestic carriage.

In time came Lord Carlton, Lord Bleers, Lord Layton, Prof. Roy Shire, Haystacks Calhoun, Argentine Rocca, Skull Murphy, not all as pretty as Gorgeous, but all with a gimmick.

This is perhaps de-emphasizing the effect that Man Mountain Dean had on wrestling. He was for years Soldier Leavitt, until he accumulated such a passel of fat that he suddenly became Man Mountain, took his wife's last name of Dean, and found himself a public attraction.

Still, Man Mountain was merely a fat showman, not a gimmick man.

There came a flurry of Masked Marvels, Golden Terrors, Monsters and the sort. But these were merely wrestlers wearing masks. The muscle still prevailed.

Nothing clever had occurred to George Wagner by 1941, at which time he spent six months in Hawaii filling engagements. During his tour in the islands, he allowed his hair to grow long. He lost a bet one day, and as loser, was required to get his long hair set in a permanent wave.

"As I sat in that beauty parlor on Waikiki Beach," he says, "a crowd of people began to gather outside the window and giggle and point at me. Wherever I went I attracted a crowd.

"When I got back to Hollywood, I got a velvet robe, the color of orchid. I began to wear an orchid in my lapel, I drove an orchid-colored Cadillac. The money began to roll in. I got movie offers, and when television came along, I got television offers.

"One night I used Bob Hope for my valet and I wrestled Bert Lancaster in a charity bout that raised $250,000 to build a wing on a hospital for crippled children. That's what it has done for me, the long, wavy hair, the gimmick."

And so a plain, everyday muscle man named George Wagner became Gorgeous George, a freak, an attraction, a name as commonplace as corn flakes or potato chips.

"You'll even find me," Gorgeous George said proudly, "in the Encyclopedia Britannica."

That flophouse should erect a plaque out front saying, "Gorgeous George W. Slept Here."

CHARLIE WINS A PENNANT FOR WALTER

(March, 1955)

(Playing one-day stands on a tour of major league training camps in Florida, I happened into Orlando at this opportune moment. The Brooklyn Dodgers, who had fired Charlie Dressen, were playing an exhibition game with the Washington Senators, who were now being managed by Charlie Dressen.

Since Walter Alston, manager of the Dodgers, had not made the trip, it seemed obvious that the appropriate move was to ask the man who knew the Dodger personnel next best, Charlie Dressen.

This I did, and it developed into the best move of the spring. Charlie took the bait like a lunker bass, and cut water sparing no one. The story made the wires, and it set off a sharp exchange of unpleasantries between Dodgers and Dressen. As it turned out, Charlie had such a close line on Alston's athletes that squad paring must have been somewhat embarrassing. He won a pennant with them, though, which should have offset all embarrassment.

Poor Charlie, he finished eighth, which is an old family tradition in Washington.)

ORLANDO, Fla.—This was at Tinker Field, where the Brooklyn Dodgers had gone to keep an appointment with an old flame, Charles Walter Dressen, and the Washington Nationals. Sensing that two is a crowd, Walter Alston, now approaching his second season as the successor to Dressen, had seen fit not to make this trip with the Flatbush varsity. He was down the peninsula with another unit, consisting mostly of what the baseball folk call "scrubinis."

"Well, what do you wish to know about these guys?" asked Charles Walter, sitting on a table in his new but hardly commodious office. He had been driven indoors by a sprinkle of rain. Two guests sat nearby playing rummy. A fuzzy-haired fellow appropriately called "Fuzzy" was applying generous amounts of mustard to slabs of bread in the process of preparing a ham and cheese sandwich. Two or three other miscellaneous guests charged inside addressing the small downpour with some unflattering titles.

"Let me have that," Dressen said, reaching for a Dodger roster, "and I'll pick their team for you. Got a pencil?"

Somebody handed him a pen. Dressen scanned the roster and began marking and chalking.

"This guy goes out," he said, checking the name of Joe Black, the star of his show in '52.

"Why do you say that, Charlie?"

"He just won't make it, that's all."

Dressen passed over the names of Don Bessent, Glenn Cox and Bob Darnell. He approved Carl Erskine and Jim Hughes.

"Who's this guy?" he asked. The pen stopped on the name of Sandy Koufax, the bonus baby.

"He's a bonus boy, Charlie. He's got to stay."

"Oh," Dressen said. "Well, Clem Labine stays." Then he checked off Joe Landrum, Tom LaSorda and Ken Lehman and approved Billy Loes and Russ Meyer. He paused over Bob Milliken. "I don't know about him. He needs to work."

Ron Negray was checked off, but Don Newcombe, Johnny Podres, Ed Roebuck and Karl Spooner all were hired. Charley Templeton and Pete Wojey, who served a long sentence in Mobile, also were returned to the minors.

"How many's that?" Dressen asked, and then counted off eleven. "Well, that's the pitchers. Roy Campanella's all of the catching anybody needs, if he's ready to play."

Quickly he selected Junior Gilliam, Don Hoak, Gil Hodges,

Peewee Reese, Jackie Robinson and Don Zimmer among the infielders. "I don't know too much about these guys," he said, touching the names of Chico Fernandez and Charley Neal. This second base combine up from Montreal and St. Paul has been raving hot around Florida. "Zimmer's got to stay. He can play anywhere and he hits the long ball."

The Dressen tout sheet scored Sandy Amoros, Carl Furillo, Walt Moryn, George Shuba and Duke Snider as the outfielders who'll be Brooklyn tenants this summer. "This guy," he said, checking the name of Gino Cimoli, "ought to be a big leaguer. He's a got a lot of things going for him."

Cimoli is a boy who held out last season, reported late, and then hit .306 at Montreal.

"Where's all the outfielders?" Dressen asked.

"That's all, Charlie. That's the outfield."

Dressen looked unimpressed though Furillo once led the league in hitting for him and Snider was an ace several semesters before Willie Mays discovered the Polo Grounds. "Well, that's your ball club," Dressen said. "Any questions?"

"Yeah, who's good enough to beat the Giants?"

"It's this club," Dressen said, "if they don't get their arms broke."

Outside, a group of Dodger historians inspected the Dressen-approved Dodger roster.

"He's not far from right," said the *Herald-Tribune*'s Roger Kahn.

"Black's looked good," the *Times'* Roscoe McGowen said. "How can they send him out? They've got to give the fellow a chance."

"He's looked good one time and bad one time. Charlie may be right. He must be right about Roebuck, too. He looks like he's about ready to live up to all that promise."

"They're not going to be so quick with Neal and Fernandez. Zimmer's got to stay. Charlie's right. But one of them may have to stay. They could trade Gilliam and keep Neal. He's looked great. There's no use talking about shortstop, Zimmer, Fernandez or whoever. The shortstop is Reese. It may be Reese for a long time yet."

Over in the Dodger dugout, Coach Billy Herman greeted a delegation with confidence.

"How do you figure the Dodgers can make up the difference between them and the Giants, Billy?"

"There's not too much to make up," he said. "We were just five games out. Campy's hand meant ten games to us. Erskine had a bad year. Podres was out a month. This is the ball club somebody's going to have to beat."

In the clubhouse, Jackie Robinson listened while a tattler told him about Dressen's Dodgers. "He said you'd win it if all of you don't get your arms broke, Jackie."

Robinson was both nimble and quick. "It'll be us if we do get our arms broke," he said.

Somewhere down in southeast Florida, innocent Walter Alston sat watching his scrubinis play a game, while in Orlando everybody was winning a pennant for him. It may turn out that this was a very important trip he should never have missed.

A CASEY STENGELOGUE

(March, 1959)

(*Look through the files of any man who has covered baseball awhile and you will find any number of columns such as this. They required very little writing, mostly intent listening. Notes were impossible. Casey talked too fast. Besides, he had a habit of choking up at the sight of hurrying pencils.*

On this morning, Jimmy Burns of the Miami HERALD *and I happened to catch him in private at Miller Huggins Field. The main body of the writing army lay in wait for him at Al Lang Field.*

We had him to ourselves. We inserted our dime, turned him on and sat and listened, and this is what came out—with interpolations.)

★ ★

ST. PETERSBURG, Fla.—Casey Stengel had broken out with a skin rash and rushed into the clubhouse at Miller Huggins Field for emergency treatment. The New York Yankees were playing St. Louis later in the day, but they hold the preliminaries on their own premises, which is across several stretches of palms, shuffleboard courts, green benches and octogenarians from Al Lang Field.

When Casey returned to his office, the green, low-slung dugout back of the batting cage, he played the perfect host. He invited his guests in to set a spell, then broke out in another rash, this of a vocal nature.

No one was quite sure later what started it all. The best anybody could remember was that somebody mentioned something about shortstop and Casey hydramatically shifted into gear.

"Now I've been looking at this here Richardson to see if he can play shortstop," explained the manager of the world's champions, "then if he can I've got me another three-way man. Now the only other man I've got that can make the infield is this Brickell, who has played in Triple A for two years and is a good ballplayer and could make our infield.

"Now who is the only man not here from the World Series? That would be Mr. Kubek, who is still in the Army, and so I am looking for a shortstop. I could play McDougald at shortstop. I could play Lumpe at shortstop. So you see I have possibilities."

(This means that Bobby Richardson is getting a trial at shortstop, and if he can play it to suit the chief, then he becomes the third Yankee infielder who can play multiple positions. Fritz Brickell is a round little rookie from Denver. Tony Kubek is serving out a six-month service tenure, but will report in April.)

"Now why this Siebern wants to use glasses when he learns to hit .300 without them is something I don't know. He went to see the doctor and the doctor told him he was near-sighted, but I don't think it's near-sighted, I think he just don't get the start on the ball.

"Of course Mantle is my center fielder and Bauer, they say he is getting old, but you've got to look for something like that. Slaughter, I should mention him, for he is a rosy-cheeked youth and you don't expect him to ever get old. He pinch hits good for us last year, about .300, and he is in the best condition of anybody down here, and everybody is in good condition which we write and tell them they better be three weeks before they report, to get their workouts, no matter where they live."

(This means that Norm Siebern, Mickey Mantle and Hank Bauer will play the outfield again, though Stengel is not too pleased with Siebern's defense in left. And that Enos Slaughter, 42, is also here.)

"Pitching. Well, we may not trade, but we're going to leave

two places open for trades in spite of what certain people say about not trading with us.

"Shantz is in good shape. Larsen looks very good, most of the writers say. Duren, he don't work on account of that knee operation. He just does a lot of running.

"I have another man. Nobody thinks he can make good. He don't win but two games last year. I like him from what I seen of him two years ago. Last year he had a bad season because he's got a bad arm. He come in here and tried to throw his way right on our team and he throwed too hard. He's mean. He don't like hitters.

"Oh, his name. Coates.

"Ditmar, he pitches good, but he can't get no record. I like this boy. While his record is not so good he is a good pitcher. Mr. Ford is his usual self, and don't ask me, I don't know nothing about his clauses. I just know we like to have our people in shape. If we told them to report not in shape and not look after theirselves and stay in condition we would have a camp for fat men here.

"Mr. Turley is like usual, now you mention Sturdivant. He had an accident running in the outfield at Boston last year. Somebody stepped on his leg and cut that tendon in the back here and I have to take him off the list for thirty days, then I have to go and buy another man, Trucks, to replace him, and then I buy Dickson. When he gets back there is not much he can do and he don't win but three games. But he won thirty-two in two years before, and none of our pitchers have done this since Raschi.

"If you want to know about our new men, I'll tell you. This Coates, I tell him don't strain yourself. Now this Gabler, he win nineteen games in Denver, and that is a beautiful record in that altitude. He's ready, serious, won't give up. This Bronstad is a good looker, too."

(This means that Whitey Ford, Don Larsen, Bob Turley, Art Ditmar and Tom Sturdivant, who had the bad year, will be the lead pitchers again; that Virgil Trucks and Murry Dickson are still here; that Ryne Duren is recovering from a knee operation, and that the Yankees need a relief pitcher; that Jim Coates, John Gabler and Jim Bronstad are good rookies; and that "certain party" is Frank Lane, who has been urging a trade boycott of the Yankees.)

"Nobody has got two catchers like our catchers. Blanchard is hurt now, but Bill Dickey is working on him and he has done a great job. We got nine catchers in the league which Dickey has taught and we have traded, like this Berberet and Try-andos, so he is a good teacher but we can't tell about Blanchard for he is hurt."

(This means that Yogi Berra is still a catcher, but that he will share again with Elston Howard, and that both will play the outfield some. Blanchard, up from Denver, will be the third man.)

"Now Chicago has the best chance to beat us out with their young ball players and their second base combination, Fox and that little shortstop. Now I like Detroit. The best part of their ball club is the experienced third baseman and the experienced shortstop.

"Cleveland is better, of course, and I like this about Boston. They got five good hitters, Williams, Wertz, Runnels, and he just loses the batting race on the last day, and Jensen and Malzone.

"Are we stronger than last year? Well, we'd better be stronger, for everybody else in the league is stronger."

(This means that the Yankees will win the pennant their way again, but that Stengel is courteous enough to acknowledge the presence of seven other ambitious, but bloodless, rivals.)

PROF. WALTON'S BASEBALL UNIVERSITY

(February, 1961)

(Tubby Walton is a third-degree legend around the South. He dates back to the days when most major league baseball clubs had no more than two or three scouts. Each scout had his own spread of "bird dogs" and Tubby was one of these.

He operated on a shoestring and collected his small fee only when he turned up a likely find. This was before the ridiculousness of the bonus. Little money ever changed hands between scout and player. Kids were looking for work.

In the course of this pursuit, Tubby came up with what he insists was the first baseball school, and the stories of his "university," as he called it, and some of its famous alumni are all a part of the legend.

Tubby has long since been out of baseball, so indignant was he when bonus money came in and spoiled his game of salesmanship. Now he sells insurance. I ran into him on Peachtree Street one day and we fell into a fit of nostalgia, and this resulted.)

It had been too long since I had seen Tubby Walton—with his clothes on, at least. He had been on the last occasion, if my memory is accurate, running around the Health Club at the YMCA wrapped only in a Turkish towel, which is a new achievement for the towel industry.

Once upon the days of Herbert Hoover's poverty-stricken regime, there wasn't a towel made that would have spanned the breadth of William Hewlett Walton. In contrast to the economy of the times, he was as big as a side of beef, and it was then that he earned his degree as Tubby.

"Nobody ever ast my name befo'," Tubby said in his native tongue, "except the revenue man and a traffic cop. Ain't ten people in Atlanta know I'm William Hewlett Walton."

Tubby got so fat because he ran a restaurant called "Tubby's Home-Cooked Meals."

When his weight blew up to 350 pounds, and when he found he was giving away more meals at the back door than he was selling up front, he closed up his kitchen and quit.

Those were the days when the baseball scout was a rare breed, and Tubby was one of them, and indeed a rare breed. No major league club kept a roster of over two or three salaried scouts. All the rest were "bird dogs," whose reports usually consisted of nothing more than a hastily scrawled note on tablet paper with a carpenter's pencil, or in a case of urgency, a collect telephone call.

Tubby's scouting practices went beyond the general limit of his contemporaries' efforts. He was a progressive. He organized what he insists was the first baseball school in the history of mankind and attracted the young geniuses to come unto him.

"This was 1928," he said. "You show me a baseball school befo' that and I'll eat Branch Rickey's fedora.

"One day at my modest little restaurant, Bird Hope come in for lunch. He was the coach at Fulton High School, which was at Whitehall and Trinity then. 'Tubby's Home-Cooked Meals' was just down the street.

"'I got a little boy that can hit a curve ball,' Bird said. He talked with a little whine.

"'Ain't no boy can hit a curve ball, Bird,' I said.

"'This boy kin,' Bird said. 'Look a little like a Indian and kin hit a curve ball.'

"'Bring him out,' I said. I ast him to bring him out to Tubby Walton's Baseball University, of which I was the president. President of a university and couldn't read or write. It was located out at Almand Park. Our campus was a skin diamond and a chicken-wire backstop.

"So Bird bring him out. I got this pitcher who was sort of mean. Later got in jail. I tole him to knock this Indian down and then curve him. This mean boy low-bridged him, then that Indian-looking boy hit the next curve ten miles.

"I tole Bird I'd take him without any further examination. The boy tole me his name was Luke Appling. He went on out to Oglethorpe University with Frank Anderson, and I kept watching him and I finally signed him for the Crackers. Rell Spiller give him $1,000 and me $500.

"Luke later sent me $500 after he got to the major leagues. He shouldn't of done it. I lost it in the restaurant.

"I had this boy in my university named Leroy Waldrop. He tole me, 'Mistuh Walton, a boy out in Clayton County I know can hit anybody.'

" 'Ain't nobody kin hit anybody, Leroy,' I said.

" 'This boy kin,' Waldrop said, 'but he can't get away. His daddy's got him plowing.'

"I told Waldrop to get that boy up to the university at 9 o'clock the next morning and I'd let him be our guest for a spell. He showed up the next morning, lookuh heah, wearing tennis shoes, white duck pants and old cap. I told him to get a bat and have a swing.

"He reached back and picked up a bat and never even looked at it. All my athletes always looked at the label. If it wasn't Babe Ruth or Al Simmons or Jimmy Foxx, they wouldn't hit with it.

"Hugh Casey was pitching. I told ol' Hughie to bear down, and lookuh heah, this tall, lean ol' plowboy hit a line drive off him, and kept hitting 'em.

"Kid Elberfield was the dean of men, and I told him we better drive this boy out to his house personally and talk to his daddy ourselves.

"I remember just as we drove up the last hill before we got to the farm, the boy said, 'Mistuh Walton, get Pa to let me plow and play baseball, too.'

"His daddy turned out to be a school teacher. I'd never signed anybody that could read before. He sat on that porch and rocked and read every word in that contract.

" 'It sounds like he's joining the chain gang,' his daddy said.

" 'It does sound like that,' I said, 'but they'll pay him for his work. They don't pay on the chain gangs.'

"I signed the boy and his name was Cecil Travis. I took him to Chattanooga and Joe Engel paid me $300. Cecil never got a dime."

THE MANY MOODS OF MAUCH

(Selected for "Best Sports Stories of the Year—1961")

(May, 1961)

(*One night in New Orleans in 1953, Gene Mauch and I sat up until 3 A.M. discussing the mistakes he had made as a 27-year-old manager of the Atlanta Crackers. He had been rushed into the genius business too soon, and now he realized it, but he would study some more and he would return to managing in time.*

He was a cinch to manage in the major leagues. His mind reacted to baseball situations with enviable instinctiveness. It was only a matter of restraining his emotions.

Now he was a manager in the major leagues. I was in Cincinnati researching a story for SATURDAY EVENING POST *on Vada Pinson, the outfielder. I got there just in time to see Mauch strike a match to all his good intentions, and to see Crosley Field turned into a patch of mayhem on a Sunday afternoon when he threw one of his good old-fashioned fits.*)

★ ★

CINCINNATI—There was a strikingly familiar photograph of Gene Mauch in the sports section of the Cincinnati *Enquirer* Sunday morning. He had Bill Jackowski, a National League umpire, by the ear and was filling it full of complaint after his pitcher, Jack Meyer, had been called out on an interference play.

It was a pose that Mauch struck so frequently in the year 1953, while employed as manager, second baseman and umpire baiter by the Atlanta Crackers.

This bit of Saturday negotiation, however, was merely a rehearsal for what was to follow Sunday afternoon at Crosley Field. Under the management of Mauch, the Philadelphia Phillies and the Cincinnati Reds were concluding a four-game series with a doubleheader.

On Saturday, the Phillies had broken a nine-game winning streak for the Reds, and on Sunday they were rubbing their noses in the dirt. As the eighth inning of the first game arrived, Philadelphia was leading Cincinnati, 9–1.

Raul Sanchez, a Cuban as thin as a soda straw, was pitching in relief for the Reds. He walked Tony Taylor. John Callison and Ken Walters singled. A run had scored and Ted Lepcio came to bat.

Sanchez, who is a sidearm pitcher, was wild with a curve and hit Lepcio on the rump. This loaded the bases. Cal Neeman, the catcher, was next and Sanchez hit him on the rump, too. Sanchez missed Joe Koppe, the shortstop, four times and walked him.

Gene Conley, pitcher by summer, rebounder for the Boston Celtics by winter, was the next batter. He is long and lank and does not offer an inviting target, but Sanchez hit him, also on his inconspicuous rump.

Conley started slowly toward first base, and as he did, this figure wearing No. 32 on the back burst out of the Phillies' dugout and charged the mound. Then, sirs and mams, the damnedest baseball brawl you ever saw broke out.

No. 32 was five-foot, ten-inch Gene Mauch, who had had a craw full, and who had gone to the aid of his defenseless six-foot, eight-inch pitcher. Fist fights broke out all over Crosley Field and turned into wrestling matches. Ball players, coaches and umpires were wallowing all about the place in rare and sometimes ludicrous forms of combat, and it was at least ten minutes before the riot subsided.

Before it was over, Billy Martin, former welterweight champion of the American League, was led off the field bloody and torn. Robin Roberts, customarily a disciple of peace, and Frank

Robinson, the Cincinnati first baseman, had squared off like Peter Jackson and Bob Fitzsimmons.

It was purely coincidental that before this game, Mauch had explained in deliberate and forthright manner his new devotion to patience, mildness and all forms of temperance.

"The best thing that ever happened to me was that year of managing in Atlanta," he said. "It took that to teach me how much I didn't know about baseball. Then I went back to playing for five more years to learn.

"I found out, for one thing, that you can't chew out a bunch of Double A ball players because they don't play like big leaguers. I learned to sit back and watch some before I made a move."

Now in the Phillies' clubhouse, a somewhat sheepish and a somewhat serious Mauch met a rather amused press with a dour countenance.

"Well, what would you do?" he asked. "They knock down three out of four of your guys and the umpires say nothing to the pitcher. The next time they throw at the head and they hurt somebody bad. How much you gonna take of this?"

In his short time as a major league manager, Mauch has gradually won respect complimentary to a man of his position. "It wasn't sudden and easy," Sandy Grady, the Philadelphia columnist said. "For the first two or three days he didn't say much. He'd just look at you every time you asked a question, like you were a subversive agent."

Of course the conditions under which Mauch became manager of the Phillies were rather ripe with involvement. Eddie Sawyer developed a deep-seated grouch against the Phillies and gave in to a violent urge to get out the day after the season opened.

That night, in a motel room in Pompano Beach, Florida, Mauch's telephone rang him out of a deep sleep. He had the Minneapolis ball club there for an exhibition series with Dallas.

"It was John Quinn," Gene said. "He said, 'A friend of mine wants to know if you're interested in managing a major league club.'

"He said, 'Are you interested; I want to know that first.'

"I said, 'Who is it, the Phillies?'

"That's the way it happened. I took the job right there."

There was a story the other day that Mauch had called in his athletes, who have a reputation for playboyism, and laid down the law. That varies a bit from the official version.

"I didn't want to walk in here new and start off with a set of rules that might be needed," Mauch said. "I wanted to see for myself what was necessary and what wasn't, see what kind of fellows these guy were.

"I found out and then I made up my rules and I posted them, that's what took place. Now they know what I expect of them."

Patient, temperate, reserved, mild, objective, humanitarian— all of these virtues possessed our young man until Sunday afternoon in the eighth inning of the first game. Then the hell with all that. He wasn't going to take nothing off nobody no more.

He is still learning and this was one more of those lessons.

THE VIEW FROM VINEGAR BEND

(December, 1951)

(*This was composed in Shep Baxter's store and dispatched to Western Union in Mobile by a man driving a dump truck. I had gone to southwest Alabama to write a story for* SPORT *Magazine on Wilmer Mizell, a left-handed pitcher who offered the major leagues something fresh in personality as well as possessing a better-than-average degree of promise at his trade.*

I come from a country town myself—Denton, North Carolina, the home town of a left-handed Cardinal of another age, Max Lanier. But to go to Vinegar Bend, Alabama, was going about as far back in the country as a fellow could go without a guide and a compass.

On top of that, I was shocked to discover that Wilmer was a phony. He actually didn't live in Vinegar Bend. He merely got his mail there.)

VINEGAR BEND, Ala.—There is such a place. You find it forty-four miles northwest of Mobile on the left bank of the Escatawpa River and on the tracks of the Gulf, Mobile & Ohio Railroad. A marker on Highway 45 points down an unpaved road to the settlement, once a booming sawmill center of 3,000, but now reduced to thirty-five citizens and a postmark that is gaining phenomenally in national popularity.

This was not an expedition to establish the existence of Vinegar Bend, but to disinter its most famous addressee, Wilmer Mizell. Wilmer gets his mail at Shep Baxter's combination village store-service station-post office, but he doesn't live in Vinegar Bend. Actually, he doesn't even live in Alabama, but 200 yards across the Mississippi line in the farmhouse where he was born. It is in this remote region that he buries himself after each baseball season is done.

Mizell became "Vinegar Bend" when the St. Louis Cardinal scout who discovered him at a tryout camp in Biloxi, William (Buddy) Lewis, started corresponding with him. The postmark infatuated Lewis, and when Mizell reported to Albany for the 1949 Georgia-Florida League season, he came labeled "Vinegar Bend."

He has since become a very important person, a left-handed Dizzy Dean to the Texas League and the most exciting pitching personality in the Cardinal organization since Jay Hanna h'isted hisself from Houston to St. Louis. They are similar in only one respect—pitching. Dean threw hard and struck out a lot of people, and so does Mizell. Diz was a braggart. This tender 21-year-old talks a lot, but it's the unaffected conversation of a country boy doing what comes naturally, just the way he took up pitching.

"One of my cousins moved back to the country from Mobile," Vinegar says, and all the time he talks there's a coal black cowlick bobbing up and down over his forehead and he's grinning like a school kid called on to recite on parents' day, "and he got us all interested in baseball. We got us up a team and cleared us off a patch of broom sage and made us a playing field. We called ourselfs the Long Branch Rebels, and we was just a bunch of fellers out there farmin'—pea-patchin', we call it—and turpentinin' and trying to feed ourselfs.

"I was the whole pitchin' staff. I started ever game and won eighteen and tied two. We was invited up to a tournament that they scheduled us to play two times in one day in, because they figured with one pitcher we couldn't make it. Well, I pitched eighteen innings that day and we won both of 'em and the tournament. We had a free-for-all afterwards, and we won that, too."

The team was made up mostly of Vinegar Bend and his relatives, a brother and some cousins. They talked him into visiting the Biloxi camp in September of 1948, but he'd go only if they'd go with him. Vinegar had pitched to only three batters when a fearful hurricane frothed up the Gulf Coast and sent everybody scurrying for home. Lewis had been impressed, though, and he was around for the ceremony when Vinegar got his diploma from Leakesville (Miss.) High School the next spring. He signed him for $500 and put him on the train to Albany.

"I'll never forget when he arrived," says Sheldon Bender, who was a manager at Albany that year. "He didn't have glove, shoes or sweatshirt. He was just there. I gave him two uniforms, one for home and one for the road, and he handed back the road suit. 'I won't need but one,' he told me. For the first month he was up at 5 o'clock every morning walking around the hotel. He was used to getting up to milk the cows at 5.

"He didn't know anything about pitching. He called a curve a 'crook' and he knew nothing about how to throw one. He'd just been throwing hard and getting a natural break. He didn't know there was a special grip."

Vinegar Bend was kept around a couple of weeks before he was allowed in a game, and then away from home. "We didn't dare risk exposing him in Albany." Eventually, he developed into a winner and a strikeout artist that came near spoiling Albany as a baseball town. "He was the difference between a 3,000 and a 1,000 house," Bender says. "Now everybody in Albany is expecting another Mizell, and his kind comes along about once in twenty years."

Mizell moved up to Winston-Salem, won seventeen and lost seven, set a league record when he struck out seven in a row as he fanned eighteen one night and otherwise fascinated the customers on the side winning cow-milking contests, riding jack-asses around the ball park and singing his unabridged version of "I'm a Country Boy."

For these, and other reasons, he was called in to spend last spring with the Cards at St. Petersburg. He so completely charmed the big league set with his infectious ways that they saturated the wires with serenades in his behalf. Nothing attracted them more than his sprawling gait, unquestionably developed from several seasons of straddling furrows in the wake of a mule.

"I never built up any hopes of staying last year," Vinegar says. "But I'm ready now. I don't care about getting rich, but I'd like to make some money for Grandmaw. Her and my uncle raised me because my daddy died when I was a kid. Each year I ask about big money and they tell me that comes later. I'm gonna tell 'em this time that later's done here."

Some of the Immortals

BOTH MASTER AND SLAVE

(September, 1955)

(*There isn't much to say about this column. It is quite natural that in Atlanta a sports editor would have occasion to write of Robert Tyre Jones Jr. now and then.*

This was a special occasion, observance of the twenty-fifth anniversary of his Grand Slam. The dinner in his honor was a sprawling affair, covering the entire gymnasium floor at the Athletic Club. There were stretches heavily emotional, but it was Bob himself who loosened up the audience when he stood to acknowledge all these things.

Its most poignantly impressive moment came when his lawyer-father stood to say a few things that only a father can say of a son. For a few minutes Bobby became a boy again, and his father figuratively patted him on the head and told him what a fine boy he had been. A father with four boys of his own can appreciate this kind of sentimental gesture a little more than anybody else, I guess.)

This is about Bobby Jones, who will never be Bob, written on the twenty-fifth birthday of his Grand Slam of golf. Of his Impregnable Quadrilateral, as [O.B.] Keeler called it. I wasn't there. I have never seen him hit a golf ball. I am merely a guy who arrived after the show was over and the performers had gone home.

I know him now as an attorney who gets about laboriously and who has learned so gracefully to live with his burden. Perhaps more than anything else I admire him for this grace, for adjusting his athletic being to the limitations required by his cruel fate.

Tuesday evening his golf friends gathered and banqueted with him at the Atlanta Athletic Club. There were some speeches, and the reminiscences were sweet to the ears, even if they didn't belong to you. It was twenty-five years ago to the day that Bobby had defeated Gene Homans, 8 and 7, in the final round of the National Amateur at Merion Cricket Club in Ardmore, Pennsylvania.

He had won the British Amateur, the British Open and the U.S. Open. This was the fourth side of the quadrilateral. Even then the world was assured it would never happen again. The progress of golf has made this one of the cinches of all history.

Homans himself is important to the story only in that he was the victim marched in for the kill. True, the year before he and Bobby had tied for the medal in the National Amateur. But Homans was a cut below the great players of the time, George Von Elm, Jess Sweetser, Chick Evans and Francis Ouimet. Homans was not a stylish player, but is characterized by Bobby as "one who got a lot out of the game he had."

Incidentally, Homans is no longer able to play himself. He has arthritis of the feet. He came from New Jersey and he has settled there in the insurance business formed by his father.

It isn't easy to comprehend the retirement from competition of an athletic youth of 28. But Bobby had been plotting his retirement at least four years in advance.

"I started looking for a good chance to quit for several years before," he said. "I guess I really decided back in 1926, when I got around to the National Amateur and couldn't get nervous about it. Von Elm beat me in the finals. That's when I felt I should begin to look for a way to quit, when I couldn't get nervous about it.

"I had to be nervous to play my best when I was playing competitively. You don't win playing relaxed. The muscles are relaxed but you're nervous. That's the way it's got to be. Three or four years after I quit I played in my first Masters. I was nervous, but it hurt my game. It's perfectly obvious why. I wasn't keyed for the tension of competition any more.

"Am I amazed at what golf has done for me? I guess you could put it that way. I've seen it do a lot for fellows like Sarazen, Hagen, Diegel and a lot of others. I guess it's sort of like Emerson and the mousetrap, isn't it?

"We lived those days intensely, Keeler and I. I guess when I got out I missed the tension. There's nothing in the world more fun than a real tight golf match. But I'd get wrought over the things, fume and swear at myself for two or three days after a tournament I hadn't won. By the time I was 28, I'd had fourteen or fifteen years of playing tournaments. I was taking so much out of myself being keyed up and intent on winning. I felt the punishment I was taking was out of proportion to the importance of the thing."

In all his days, Bobby took just one bad beating. The welts have grown out under the soothing balm of time. If it is bitter to him now, there are no outward signs. Newspaper accounts, though, indicate he was cut deeply when Walter Hagen trounced him, 11 and 10, in a special match between the best professional and the best amateur of the times. It was a real estate promotion match staged in the boom of Florida in 1926.

"I was just out of college a couple of years," Bobby said, "and in the real estate business with the Adairs. They bought some real estate near Sarasota and built a residential project. They built a golf course and Tommy Armour was the pro. I was sent to Florida to play the course and attract attention.

"There were other projects like it—Whitfield Estates, they called it—all over Florida, and they all had pros. Sarazen, Diegel, Farrell and Hagen were all down there. Hagen was the pro over at Pasadena, near St. Petersburg. Bob Harlow got the idea of a match between the two of us, with all the money going to Hagen, of course. A home-and-home match was arranged, eighteen holes on each course.

"So it came off. Hagen was a great fellow to play against, entertaining and a great competitor. It was the only time we ever met in match play. He finished above me in only one tournament after that, though, in the 1927 Open. Perhaps I was conscious of beating him, but I was always playing my best to beat whomever I had to beat to win."

He found in golf what he wanted. It explains why he was never able to get away from it, as if he had a choice in the matter. "When you put that much of yourself into a thing," he said, "you haven't got much left for anything else."

He was both its master and its slave.

DIMAGGIO, NINE YEARS LATER

(January, 1961)

(*In contrast to Jimmy Foxx, here is a former classic figure of baseball well adjusted to his position in retirement. Joe DiMaggio had dropped in on Atlanta for a hasty visit, but, through cocktails, dinner and conversation with a few close friends, he lived an evening with the leisure of an old plantation host.*

Here he talks of his successor in center field at Yankee Stadium, Mickey Mantle. He talks about the circumstances of his retirement. He talked about Casey Stengel, but this was off the record. The contents of the latter discussion may well be measured by the fact that a few weeks later DiMaggio accepted a spring coaching job with the new manager of the Yankees, Ralph Houk.

As far as flowers are concerned, Joe's chief interest seemed to concentrate on the flora of American feminine beauty. A few weeks later, he and ex-wife Marilyn Monroe, of the cinema, became much closer public companions again. I never did learn how ardently he pursued the suggested project of geranium growing in an eighteenth-floor apartment.)

There was a time, not so long ago either, when Joe DiMaggio would have tiptoed around the question. It was a delicate one, involving the strong boy who succeeded him as center fielder of the New York Yankees. But he never batted an eyelash.

The car moved along Cleveland Avenue toward South Expressway. Oncoming cars lighted up his face in the early evening. It was the same face, touched up only slightly by the unrelenting processes of age, and the hair wore a distinguishing fringe of grey.

"No," he said, "Mantle never has gotten the most out of himself. He's got tremendous power, from both sides of the plate; he can steal bases; he's got an arm that makes base runners respect him, but he never has put it all together at a stretch.

"He's never had a bad year. His bad years are good years for most guys. But if he'd play this game to the hilt all the way, there's no telling what he might do."

It has been, now, nine years since DiMaggio surrendered center field at Yankee Stadium to Mickey Mantle. It would have happened a year sooner, but DiMaggio was young enough when his time did come.

"I ached all over, shoulder, arms, legs and that heel," he said, referring finally to a part of his anatomy, not a cad. "When I got to spring training in 1951, it hurt me to play. I ached all over. Every time I ran a step the heel bothered me.

"I would have quit then, but I was in spring training, and you just don't quit in the middle of spring training. Dan Topping tried to get me to come back the next year, sign for the same money even to play half the games, or none at all if I didn't feel like it. But the Yankees had been good to me. I couldn't have done it that way. It was time to quit."

DiMaggio has lived sanely and soberly in the after-years of baseball. There was a flurry of exaggerated notoriety when he was engaged in wedlock with Marilyn Monroe, an event characterized by those idealists who believe in fairy tales as a modern merger of Snow White and Prince Charming.

It was a marriage of limited duration. Now Snow White is divorced again and she and DiMaggio have been reported by the gossip columnists as having tea together lately. Somehow, this question didn't come up too easily. It's sort of like asking a fellow if he has robbed any graves lately.

DiMaggio says, "We're just friends," and that seems to indicate that he'd prefer to discuss with a delegate of a sports department such scandalous matters as Mickey Mantle's talent,

Casey Stengel's talent, Ted Williams' talent and other affairs.

Now DiMaggio is 45 years old. He has a son—by his marriage to Dorothy Arnold—who is 19 and a freshman at Yale. The son is addicted to football and has made his way on his own scholarship. His daddy is proud of this.

He, Joe, lives in a suite on the eighteenth floor of the Hotel Lexington in New York, has a housekeeper seven days a week and admits that he does need some foliage around the place. This was a matter brought up at dinner, in the dimness of Atlanta Athletic Club, by his present-day employer, Val H. Monette.

"Geraniums," Monette said, "they're good indoor flowers. A little fertilizer and water them every day and they'll liven up the place. You need them. We'll send you some. Keep them watered."

He didn't say it, but you could tell that DiMaggio had had enough of gardening, horticultural and otherwise.

SEARS, ROEBUCK & WILLIAMS

(January, 1961)

(A Sears, Roebuck executive had called to drop the hint that the company had employed a sports consultant. His name was Williams, a new man from Boston. His former profession had been baseball, though he was known to have some kind of reputation as a bone-fisherman.

And so out of left field at Fenway Park into the uniform of a merchandising executive stepped Ted Williams. He had come to Atlanta for an appearance before a convention of proud Sears, Roebuck personnel who could now regard him as one of their own kind. He was very friendly and didn't seem to hate anyone, including Southern sports editors.)

A few days ago an international mail-order house announced the employment of Ted Williams, rather widely known previously as tender of left field at Fenway Park in Boston. In the narrow mind of sports, it was assumed that since Sears, Roebuck & Company was approaching its seventy-fifth year in business, Williams was being retained as the diamond anniversary attraction.

About Wednesday noon, a tall man wearing sports jacket, white shirt and blue tie and walking with a loose-jointed gait stepped off an elevator at the Biltmore Hotel with a covey of executives. Only a fellow with a program and all the numbers of the players would have been able to pick Williams out of the crowd.

The former "Splendid Splinter" had been polished up to look

like a piece of solid mahogany. He wore a name tag that said, "Ted Williams, Sports Consultant."

He was cordial, gracious, accommodating, everything a Boston sports writer would ordinarily say he isn't. Such a mention caused him to bristle.

"Those cotton-picking cotton-pickers," he didn't exactly say. "One of those guys called my daughter the other day to find out what I'd given her for Christmas. Anything to stay on my back."

The elder tier of baseball oracles has contended that Williams has changed, mellowed to the state of a pure charmer in his latter days of baseball.

"I've got two words for that," he said. Neither of which I am able to print here.

He could tell that the shirt and tie were getting some special attention. His face broke into a smile, for 99 and 44/100ths per cent of his waking life has been spent inside sport shirts.

"I'm wearing a shirt and a tie," he said, "and that's a change. But I told these people that was only in cold weather. When it's hot I'll be in sport shirts."

Now he was serious. "Here's the way I look at myself," Ted Williams said, picking up the original drift.

"I'm the same guy I always was, except I'm a little older and maybe a little smarter. I still have the same moods and I can still fly off the handle when I feel like it."

You could tell this was true. The fire still burned inside him. His eyes snapped at times. When a question aroused him, he fairly leaped to an answer, like a bass rising to assault a top-water lure.

He was smarter, too. A high-level executive of Sears, Roebuck confirmed this.

"Let me tell you that this is a hard-headed business man," said Vice President L. E. Oliver. "We didn't hire Mr. Williams for window-dressing. We think he'll be of great value in assisting these men here in our approach to the sporting goods field."

The retirement of Theodore Samuel Williams took place last fall. It almost took place a year earlier.

"Tom Yawkey didn't want me to play last season," he said.

"I'd dropped off to .254 in '59. He thought I was over the hill. He knew I'd been having trouble with my neck. I couldn't face the pitcher the way I was accustomed to. He didn't want me to ruin my record.

"I told him I'd like to come to spring training and see how it worked out. The year before I hadn't been able to play for the first month, then I got in one day against Herb Score.

"Now, I had always been able to hit Score pretty good. I went oh-for-five. I finally got my average up to .180, and then .274 at one time, but I dropped back.

"The neck was bothering me, but I thought I could still hit. I wanted one more chance at it, and I'm glad I stayed with it."

In spite of Sears, Roebuck, the non-existent J. C. Higgins et al, Williams will again appear at spring training with the Red Sox. This time he will be Prof. Williams, dean of the science of hitting.

Tom Yawkey retained him first for this position. Sears, Roebuck and Higgins came second. The two jobs won't conflict. He and his two employers have agreed on this.

One of Prof. Williams' first pupils will be his own successor at Fenway Park, a Long Island youth named Carl Yastrzemski, who played at Minneapolis. Last spring in Arizona, Williams became fascinated with Yastrzemski's manner with a bat.

"He'll take my place in left field," Ted said, "and he's liable to lead the league in hitting. He's that good. He's got an average build and hits to left center field. He's sort of a cross between Charlie Keller and Billy Goodman, and that's a pretty good combination."

Now, he was asked as the entourage moved towards the banquet hall downstairs, "Did you ever really have any serious interest in managing?"

"None," he said, emphatically. "Absolutely none. I couldn't stand all those newspaper writers around me after a game asking me why I pinch hit so-and-so, or why I didn't relieve with some other pitcher. If I'm the manager, it's none of their damned business."

He has changed, too, for when he said that word, he smiled.

AN OBITUARY FOR THE FIGHT GAME

(December, 1960)

(It was a pleasant, sunny winter day in New York. My wife and I and Harvey Hester, a very large citizen of the world who operates Aunt Fanny's Cabin in Atlanta to make up for the money he lost in the Miami Seahawks, had strolled across town for lunch with Jack Dempsey, an old friend.

Of all things and of all people, Dempsey then and there pronounced the benediction of prize fighting. He explains why, requiring no more elaboration here.

But then there was the cab driver on the way back to the Lexington Hotel. This happens to Dempsey every time he moves about in the public.

The way it seems is that Dempsey spent all his life fighting cab drivers, elevator operators, desk clerks and friends of same, except when he wasn't refereeing for them. Either that, or he converted a lot of former pugilistic dreamers into honest working men with his persuasive fists.)

★ ★

NEW YORK—This was a startling pronouncement from Jack Dempsey. He removed the smoking cigar from his mouth and said, "The fight game's dead. It was already dying, but after this Washington thing, it's washed up."

It wasn't startling because it was new. It was just that you never expected it to come from the mouth of the former heavyweight champion of the world, the man whose name remains a household phrase in this country.

We sat with some friends at a table in the front window of his restaurant on Broadway. It was early afternoon. The crippling blizzard hadn't yet struck. People rushing along the sidewalk outside, in the most sophisticated city in the world, would catch sight of him, stop and point him out to companions.

Little clots of gonkers would gather and peer through the window at him. He had his back to them, and so we talked on without paying them any mind.

"Even the heavyweights?" I asked.

"Yeah," Dempsey said. "That guy from Sweden can't fight and this guy over here can't fight and there's nobody else that can fight."

This took care rather decisively of Ingemar Johansson and Floyd Patterson. "How did boxing get in this condition, Jack?"

"The commissions," he said. "They're nothing but a bunch of guys looking for a shot at some publicity. They're politicians or front men or hangers-on or just guys that like to have a title. They never made a decision. They're afraid to. They don't run boxing. They don't know anything about it.

"That's why it's in the shape it's in and all these creeps are in it. The commissions can't do anything about that because they've got no authority in the first place."

Everything Jack Dempsey has in this world can be traced to prize-fighting. He was a boy from a poor, itinerant family of the mountainous West. Mere existence was a fight for him. When he came out of that world of poverty, everything and everybody was an enemy. When he struck, he struck to kill. That was his code.

He never wavered, even unto the last punch he ever threw. This took place in a stadium in Charlotte, North Carolina, about 1942. During the course of some refereeing appearances among the wrestlers, Dempsey had been drawn into activity through some sort of disagreement with Cowboy Luttrall that got out of hand.

Dempsey's animalistic instincts, thus aroused, brought him out of retirement for a brief fling. In Charlotte, he was matched with a wrestler named Ellis Bashara, a tough, squat man who had been a football star at Oklahoma A&M.

Bashara was young, strong and ambitious. Dempsey was close to 45 at the time, and it was easy, I suppose, for the eager youth to be fooled almost to a state of utter audacity.

Dempsey laughed at the memory. "Before the fight," he said, "this kid told me, 'I hate to knock you out, Mr. Dempsey, but I've always had an ambition to be the heavyweight champion of the world.

"'After I get you, then I'll knock out Joe Louis. But I just hope I don't hurt you.'

"He was serious, too. After we got into the ring that night, he asked the man in my corner if I was in good shape. 'I wouldn't want to hurt him for anything in the world. He was always sort of my idol.'

"The kid was still taking bows after the bell rang when I hit him. He was bleeding like a pig at the end of the first round, but he stayed with it. The second round they had to stop it. He was blood from his head to his trunks."

Dempsey was a savage that night. I'll never forget it. The night was warm. Clouds boiled overhead. A thunderstorm threatened. Lightning flashed. Dempsey's scowling countenance and vicious mood fit the weather.

Dempsey's bar and restaurant, owned in partnership with Jack Amiel, who won the Kentucky Derby with a field horse named Count Turf in 1951, is naturally a gathering place for the fight clan.

While we sat there, "Bowtie Jimmy" Bronson, a manager and handler of ancient vintage, came in. He was looking for Ned Brown, probably the most respected boxing writer of the age, also quite ancient.

Bronson's appearance reminded Harvey Hester, who also owns restaurants but seldom fights, except on short notice, of a story of Dempsey's first match with Gene Tunney. This was the bout of the long count in Chicago. Bronson had been in Tunney's corner.

"Tell Jack what you told me down in Asheville, North Carolina, several years ago, Jimmy," Harvey said.

"I said that if I had been in Dempsey's corner, I'd have jumped into the ring after the count reached ten seconds," Bronson said. "He'd either have been disqualified, or he would have won right there. Either way, he would have been spared that beating Tunney gave him in the last rounds."

Now it was after lunch and we were in a cab headed across town on 48th Street, the new Mrs. Dempsey, Mrs. Bisher, Mr. Hester and others, when somebody mentioned Jack's name.

The cab driver, fat and bald and a Bronxite to the accent, almost had a wreck whipping his head around for a view.

"Jack Dempsey?" he said. "Geez, Jack, howeryuh? You don't remember me, but . . ."

This is always a clever introduction, but this fellow did have a memory to sell.

"You refereed one of my fights out in California. Remember when you worked in Ventura? That was a long time ago, Jack. I was Johnny Delano then."

His license showed that he was Louis A. Rosetti now.

"Yeah pal," Dempsey said, "I remember Ventura."

"How about that?" said the former Johnny Delano. "Jack Dempsey in my cab and he remembers. It was the biggest pay night I ever had. It was my big fight, and you were working it. And you're in my cab and you remember it?"

"Sure pal, I remember," Dempsey said. He called off a name that Johnny Delano remembered.

Johnny turned around full face. "Geez, pal, you haven't changed a bit. Same swell guy."

We got out at the Lexington Hotel. Louis Rosetti, alias Johnny Delano, drove away exhilarated. He had a story to tell the family that night. I wondered if Jack Dempsey really had ever seen Johnny Delano in his life.

THE SACRED CARDINAL

(July, 1956)

(*Frank Lane had almost committed political suicide in St. Louis. He not only had made a few moves in the direction of trading Stan Musial, but he had made the inordinately ridiculous blunder of talking about it.*

This caused Musial to talk of retirement. It caused the hackles on the back of his neck to arise at the slightest mention of Lane. It caused the populace of St. Louis to look for a strong rope and the highest tree limb in town, with the idea of entertaining this wooly-mouthed interloper at a hanging, namely his own.

Fortunately, Lane caught himself before he went over the cliff and the deal was undone. He found out that this fellow he was about to trade off like a used car had some stature in St. Louis. There has never been another like him in a Cardinal uniform. He wears his immortality like a well-fitting suit of clothes.)

★ ★

WASHINGTON—For all intents and purposes, they have come here to play the twenty-third major league All-Star game. But Monday was dedicated to Stanley Frank Musial, newly elected baseball player of the decade by the men who have known baseball players best. And so he sat compressed into a small space at the head table in the tight little banquet room of the Washington Touchdown Club while the harsh lights burned into him and the men of television sought in their own peculiar way to salute him.

He did not seem particularly happy in his new position of

total supremacy. A sort of a scowl was written into his face. Maybe it was boredom, for after awhile there is a limit to the thrill of adulation.

Now, though, it is different with Musial. Somehow I never thought in terms of a Musial in retreat before the advancing years. It dawns upon you, though, that he is 35 years old, that he is the senior member of the National League team, that he has been transferred from the outfield to first base because he can't make the plays he used to make from his old station.

This is a Musial who can appreciate the citations with a new warmth, for there are not many more of them to come. So the expression was not boredom. It must have been humility.

These are new days in St. Louis. It may come as a shock to you as it came to Musial, but the one they call The Man was as good as traded not so many weeks ago. A story came out of Frank Lane—"the Trading Horn of baseball," as introduced at the TD Club—that Musial was most definitely not for sale or barter.

This was to say that Lane was sorry that he ever thought in such terms, to say that there was no truth in the story that Musial was on the market, to say to Musial: "Who, me trade you? Don't be foolish."

But there was a trade in the works. It was to involve Robin Roberts and Musial. Somehow the word got to Musial. This is when the story came out that Musial was threatening to quit the game. If the trade had gone through, it's doubtful that Musial would ever have reported to his new club.

For the first time in his life, Musial knew the feeling of insecurity. No one had ever given serious thought to the prospect that there could be a St. Louis Cardinal team without Musial. They had seemed inseparable all these years.

"I'm looking forward to many more years of pleasant association with him," Lane said at Touchdown Club luncheon. This was to say, "That trade, Stan. It wasn't so."

Musial was brought in from the outfield for the fundamental reason that he can't make the plays any more out there. The arm is no longer a gun. It has paid the toll of the years. He no longer covers the ground he covered. Against his will, Stan Musial is compromising with the years.

It is not pleasant. It is more unpleasant when the second-hand word gets around that the management is disappointed in you, that there is a deal, that there really is no sentiment in baseball after all.

"This is a heartless game," a veteran writer told Musial.

"I know that," Musial said. "There's no sentiment in this game, but it hurts when you learn about it this way."

It is strange that Lane should have gone into a trading tail-spin with the Cardinals in violation of his spring philosophy.

"This is different," he told me one day in March. "This is not the White Sox of 1948. This time I have some ball players."

Then he told of asking waivers on all the White Sox as he took charge in '48, and how only two players were claimed, Howie Judson, a pitcher now in the minors, and Cass Michaels, an infielder now skulled into retirement.

"But now I've got Musial, Schoendienst, Moon, Haddix, Mizell . . ." And he named off his new Cards with pride. This was to explain his inactivity on the trading market. There was really no suitable explanation for the one deal he had already made, Brooks Lawrence and Sonny Senerchia for Jackie Collum. Lawrence is now 12–0 with the Reds, and an All-Star here today. Collum, a little man of iron, is nevertheless no starting pitcher, nor has he ever been.

"The least he could have done," groaned a St. Louis sports writer, "was wait until spring and see how Lawrence worked out. There was no rush for Collum."

Once Lane broke the seal on the new deck, however, he began to trade as if addicted. The Cardinals who were once contenders are now eight games out.

"I can't field for them or swing the bat for them or pitch for them. They've got to do something for themselves," he said grumpily at lunch Monday. This came after a bitter Sunday defeat by the Cincinnati Reds, who managed on four hits.

Lane has respected Musial only as a sacred cow whom he dare not touch for fear of the fierce reactionaries. He had discovered Musial untouchable only through the infantile process of touching. It is now quite possible that he has touched The Man into retirement when the season is done. Musial finds there is something most undesirable about the strange new feeling of insecurity.

ONE OF THE REAL CON MEN

(March, 1961)

(*Far from the madding crowd, withdrawn from the furious race of man, Red Grange had set up his camp of solitude with "Muggs," his lovely helpmate of all the years. I dropped in on him one Sunday afternoon to break up the baseball monotony of spring training, and the subject of C.C. (Cash and Carry) Pyle came up.*

Pyle was a wild-eyed promoter several decades ahead of his time. By some he was considered a scoundrel, consumed of greed and avarice. Red Grange spoke of him almost reverently. I liked best the line, "I'd never have lived if I hadn't known him."

I had run across Red at Vero Beach one afternoon when the Dodgers played the Braves an exhibition game. He came down out of the stands to speak to Charlie Dressen, a former quarterback himself, and in so doing, found himself standing next to Art Fowler, the pitcher.

This reminded me of Fowler's aversion to running, regarded by all baseball managers as necessary to keep a pitcher's legs strong. And I recalled the case that Fowler had once presented against it, because it included reference to Grange.

"If running would make you a pitcher," he said, "Red Grange would have been the greatest pitcher that ever lived, and he never won a game.")

INDIAN LAKE ESTATE, Fla.—In what a mountain boy would define as a back porch in a tropical retreat, Red Grange sat in a state of Florida relaxation. Loosely translated, this means that he wore walking shorts, a light, open-necked

sports shirt and his position in the chair suggested putting off
until tomorrow what one might have done today.

This broad veranda was backed up to a lawn so green it might
have been dyed, and which rolled gently down to one of many
man-made lagoons that feed off Indian Lake, the local father of
waters.

A kindly afternoon sun bathed the premises with a caressing
heat. The rays bounced off the dazzling white finish of the house
with a sort of halo effect.

Next door, a former clerk of the Supreme Court raked his
lawn. Across the lagoon, a retired Army colonel backed out the
driveway and slowly drove away. Fifteen minutes later another
automobile came down the palm-laced driveway.

"Life bats along at a furious pace down here, I reckon," a
transient ventured.

This was obviously life in its most pronounced form of organized isolation. A superb kind of quiet prevailed, the kind over
which you can hear the mating call of the male bass to the
female bass fifteen fathoms under.

"I guess it does seem kind of dull around here, unless you've
been living in Miami, with sports cars racing along your street,
and parties going until early morning, and standing in line at
the first tee waiting to get on the course," Red said.

"Muggs and I were driving through here on the way from
Miami north a few years ago. We saw this place and it looked
nice and quiet and uncongested. We took down the name and
wrote for literature, exactly the way you wouldn't expect a real
estate prospect to behave," Red said.

"We liked it and bought this place on the lagoon and we've
been living here about three years now. It's great, and if you've
been choking to death in the congestion of Miami, it's even
greater."

The location is about eighteen miles east of Lake Wales, in
central Florida, with about 50 miles of swamp, palmetto, cab-
bage palm, and rich, black muck between here and Vero Beach,
nearest civilization to the east. It took a brave man to hack out

a settlement here, but the developers obviously had carefully calculated the lust for privacy of such a man as Red Grange, his eardrums bruised by years of noise and the clamor of the phony, the celebrity hound and even the sincere.

Had it not been for a rare specimen of the '20s named Charlie Pyle, the indestructible football legend of Red Grange might not have been so well preserved.

C. C. Pyle was a con man, a manipulator, a gambler who lost almost as many fortunes as he ever made, but first and foremost, a promoter. He operated theaters in Champaign, Illinois, while halfback Harold Grange of Wheaton, Illinois, ran for the University of Illinois until he was the most widely known undergraduate of the era.

One night, near the close of the 1925 football season, as Red started in to see a movie, the lady in the ticket booth said, "Mr. Pyle would like to see you in his office."

"When I walked in," Red said, "Charlie said, 'Red, how'd you like to make $100,000?'"

"'Who do I have to kill?'" I said.

"He wanted me to sign a personal services contract, play pro football, make a movie, sign testimonials, all sorts of money deals.

"I thought it over for a while, and in time I signed. No matter what the public may have thought of Charlie Pyle, I'll say this:

"He did everything he said he would do. He never lied to me. He was like a second father to me. But if he had taken me for anything, it would have been worth it. I've never met another man like him. I wouldn't have lived if I hadn't known him."

With two incredibly ludicrous coast-to-coast running hikes, called the "Bunion Derby," Pyle constructed for himself a lasting memorial in the American mind. He promoted a foot race from Los Angeles to New York in 1927, and a return trip in 1928.

"It was fantastic," Red said. "They came from all over the world, Estonia, India, Iceland, Russia, England, France, everywhere. Some were crackpots and some were runners. Over 300 started and 55 finished, and it took something like 67 days.

"We had a traveling community that jumped from town to town to take care of the runners. It took a lot of overhead, but Charlie sold over $250,000 worth of programs the first race. The prize money was $55,000, and he did all right on it. He lost his shirt on the return race the next year.

"I was a judge in the first race, but my contract with him ran out, and I dropped off in Chicago, so I actually saw just half the first race. What Charlie had in mind was the greatest sports event in the world. He loved acclaim, and that was his way of figuring to get it.

"This is the way I'll always remember Charlie Pyle: Black topcoat with satin lapels, derby hat, spats and a cane and carrying a pair of light gloves. He dressed like a dandy. Even when he didn't have but a dime in his pocket, he dressed like a millionaire.

"He always said, 'It's not how much money you've got. It's how you look.' He died in 1939, and they say he was broke, but he wasn't. He'd just made a new pile. He didn't live long enough to lose it."

POP WARNER: THORPE VS. NEVERS

(March, 1954)

(*Here was a paradox. Sports writers had acclaimed Jim Thorpe the "Athlete of the Half-Century," but his own football coach called him only the second best player he had ever coached.*

One morning a few months before this was written, I had had breakfast in Cincinnati with Pop Warner and he had said the same thing in essence. It came up now on the death of Thorpe, who had become a charity case in his latter years.

This tragically shabby climax to the life of a great athlete only emphasized what Coach Warner had said. I believe you'll find that he drives home his point with withering effectiveness.)

★ ★

There are two reasons Glenn (Pop) Warner has never considered Indian Jim Thorpe the greatest football player he ever coached. Both have to do with what makes a man tick, as against the ability a man has at his disposal. For how he used what he had, Ernie Nevers was his man. I have it in the great teacher's own careful handwriting.

"My answer has always been that I considered Ernie Nevers and Jim Thorpe the greatest I ever coached, but that I considered Nevers the better player because of his great dependability and because he gave everything he had in playing ability in every game, whether his team was behind or had a commanding lead."

The letter was composed nearly three years ago when Coach Warner, now retired to his home in Palo Alto, California, made his contribution to a football series I conduct for the *Saturday Evening Post*, "The Best Player I Ever Coached." Pop Warner was the leadoff man in 1951, and he risked public challenge when he picked a workhorse fullback over an all-time all-America halfback. Thorpe's death Saturday came just two years after sports writers recognized him as not only a great football player, but the greatest athlete of the 1900–1949 half-century.

Nevers came out of Willow Grove, Minnesota, to play for Warner at Stanford. He was a great inside runner, place-kicker, punter and passer, as versatile as Thorpe, but lacking the Indian's elusiveness on the outside. In 1925, Nevers was a sweeping choice for All-America, thirteen years after Thorpe had been Warner's meal-ticket at Carlisle Institute in Pennsylvania.

Both later crashed the baseball major leagues, and the similarity unfortunately continued. Neither was ever a success. Nevers pitched three seasons for the St. Louis Browns and won six games. Outfielder Thorpe tried for parts of six seasons to master the curve, the good pitch that Nevers didn't have. He busted National League pitching for a .330 average in 1919, but the Boston Braves were not impressed. They returned him to the minors the next year and he never appeared in the majors again.

Thorpe's one contribution to National League History had to do with the only double no-hit game ever pitched in the majors. His dribbling infield single in the tenth inning scored the only run in the legendary match between Fred Toney and big Jim Vaughn on May 2, 1917. Toney of Cincinnati, who died this month in Nashville, was the winner and Vaughn of the Cubs the loser after going nine innings without surrendering a hit.

Baseball was the only sport to which Thorpe gave everything he had. It demanded less concentration. It also paid money. It was also the one sport in which he didn't have enough to be great.

After Thorpe's careless ways, the chance to coach a great athlete with Nevers' All-America attitude brought Warner his supreme satisfaction. Penn once defeated the great Carlisle team by a touchdown scored on a long pass in Thorpe's territory.

"Thorpe was playing safety on defense," wrote Warner, "and it looked as though he should have intercepted or at least knocked that pass down. After the game I asked him about it.

" 'Oh, that long pass to Miller?' he said. 'Sure, I could have kept him from catching it. I saw him running down the field and the long pass he was trying to get under, but I never thought he could get to it.' "

Such shocks have caused sudden death in the case of other coaches, but the rock-bound Warner is now in his eighties and still eating heartily.

Thorpe preferred any other route to the end zone except the short-cut through the line, and one Saturday after a scoreless first half with Syracuse on a muddy field Warner called for a change of attack.

"Jim's end runs did not go very well under the adverse conditions. Between halves I told him and the team that the ball and the footing were so slippery that line plays should be used, and to cut out the wide runs.

"Jim remarked, 'What's the use of running through them when you can run around them?' Thorpe and the team took my advice and scored thirty-three points in the second half. After that, Jim took greater pleasure in hitting the line more often."

The big Indian was never bound by training rules, but the intense Nevers faithfully took pride in conditioning. "I don't want to say anything not of a laudable nature about Jim," Warner said, "but he was at times a bit off the beam in observing training rules."

Who can say that Thorpe would have been a greater athlete with Nevers' attitude? Perhaps it was his passive disposition that made him the great athlete he was. Surely he has the record on his side, for no other athlete has even been an All-America football player, an Olympic champion, and a major league football and baseball player.

In conclusion, Warner made his point as niftily as Thorpe ever made a downfield run.

"If you were a spectator," he said, "you'd take Thorpe. If you were a coach, you'd take Nevers.

"I was the coach."

A RELIC OF OLD INDIAN DAYS

(May, 1957)

(*Bob Feller stopped in Atlanta on one of these commercialized missions to save the nation's youth from degradation. He had retired from pitching, though it is plainly written between the lines here that he hadn't completely reconciled himself to such a senile condition.*

Of all the great major league baseball players I've known, Feller was less easy to warm up to than most. He was not close-mouthed. He talked at a worthy pace. He was not testy. He had no hatred for any race or union, such as sporting authors.

It seems that there was something condescending about him, maybe the tone of his voice, the tilt of his head, or his cock-sure stride. At any rate, of all the times I talked with him, this is the only occasion on which I felt I came away with enough material for a column, and of course, by this time he was working at public relations.)

Bob Feller is not much for mush and sentimentality. Had he been, he would have hired out to some team in the major leagues this season as a living, breathing relic and let the curtain fall slowly on the last quarter-century's greatest pitching attraction.

He could be pitching for a number of teams in the American or National leagues. They clamored for him in the winter. He could be pitching still for Cleveland, and with Mike Garcia and Bob Lemon in retreat, he might be working prominently in the Indian pitching routine.

"Kerby Farrell said he wanted me back, so I hear," Feller said

Tuesday in the plushness of a Biltmore Hotel suite. "Maybe he did. I'd like to have pitched some more. I think that if I'd have paid more attention to condition and less to public relations I might be pitching full blast yet.

"But there was nothing to be proved. If I'd have had a chance to break some of Walter Johnson's records, I'd have stayed with it. I think that I could have pitched until I was 40 or 42. Say that I had, what then?

"I'd have got a late start on my business. This opportunity wouldn't have been there then. And if I'd have pitched for some other club can you imagine what it would have been like, going back to Cleveland? Like mashed potatoes warmed over."

It became a matter of controversy in Cleveland last winter. Should the Indians keep Feller and let him live out his last active days gracefully? Should they release him and bring down the house of public sentiment on Hank Greenberg's already bloodied head? Or should they make a comfortable bed for him in the front office?

The solution to this perplexing problem was furnished by Motorola, the radio and appliance manufacturing people. They hired Feller to carry the word of baseball from city to city and youth to youth, and he was making his delivery to the Boys Clubs of Atlanta Tuesday.

His form, you might say, was still the unmistakably stylish form of the Feller of the mound.

"I am not a front office man," Feller said. "I worked hard for the players' pension plan. In fact, we held one of our biggest meetings right here in Atlanta, at the 1953 minor league convention. Commissioner Ford Frick was going to kill the pension until we got into action here.

"I think the players ought to have a voice in electing the commissioner. I think there ought to be some revisions in the player draft. I think there ought to be some modification of the reserve clause.

"So you see I wouldn't have gone very big in the front office."

Twenty years ago last July 19 Feller broke into the major

leagues. He appeared in relief against Washington in Griffith Stadium and threw his first pitch behind the batter, Red Kress, then walked him.

He walked the pitcher, Monte Weaver. Then he retired Ben Chapman, Buddy Lewis and Joe Kuhel. To Lewis went the select honor of becoming the first of Feller's 2,531 strikeout victims.

Almost everything good that can happen to a pitcher happened to Feller. No-hitters, strikeout records, many victories, many citations and much money. But he did not win a World Series game, a thought, however, that has not embittered him.

He was ignored by Manager Al Lopez as the Indians blew four in a row to the Giants in '54.

"I thought," he said, "that Lopez would not pitch Garcia, not so much that he would pitch me. I'd always handled the Giants pretty good in the spring. They were a fastball-hitting club, and I threw them a lot of sinkers, sliders and change-ups. Garcia was a fast-ball pitcher, and they clobbered him."

It is entirely probable that Feller jimmied the barnstorming lock after the '46 season. This was the year the Cards and Dodgers had a playoff for the National League pennant.

This was also a wealthy postwar year. Money was everywhere. The natives hungered for the sight of their war heroes as athletes again. Feller and his troops hit the Midwest and Far West as soon as the season was over and the public stormed the gates.

"This was the year," Feller said, "that the umpires made more in the World Series than the losing team. The umpires drew $2,500. The Red Sox got about $2,400 apiece for a seven-game series and the Cards about $3,400. They have small parks in St. Louis and Boston, you know.

"Well, I paid Stan Musial $7,200, though the World Series kept him from joining us until we'd reached Los Angeles. They overflowed the stadium that day, incidentally. Ten thousand couldn't get in. Bob Lemon's brother was almost crushed in a stampede at the gate. That's the way the money was those days.

"Musial said in speeches several times that winter that he

made almost twice as much barnstorming as he did in the World Series. This didn't set too well with the executives. They could see players preferring to barnstorm than to play in the World Series. So they made that rule—no barnstorming until ten days after the season closed."

It was just as well. That was the prime year. Barnstorming never was the same again. The natives blew their war profits fast and turned to such innocent backroom pastimes as fixing basketball games, doping horses and embezzling.

And in competition to these crude elements, Feller barnstorms again, setting the puritan example.

THE FUTILE PURSUIT OF PANCHO

(April, 1957)

(*Everybody has something to say here but the star of the story. Speedy Pancho Gonzales, the world's greatest tennis player, was too elusive to be found.*

He was on his way to Atlanta for another stop on that professional tour that must be a boring ordeal to him. He and Jack Kramer were, as usual, having a public debate about the ethics of their arrangement. Pancho claimed he was being robbed. Kramer claimed Pancho was robbing him.

Pancho, therefore, was having very little to do with telephones, unless he placed the call. As it turned out, I think I enjoyed writing this more than if I'd have located Pancho. I had a couple of sessions with him later, but I failed to find any improvement in what he had to stay. As a player of tennis, though, he was the supreme of the time, no doubt about it.)

★ ★

This has been an interesting chase. It began, as I recall foggily, of a Wednesday morning. It was most unusual in that it was fun without the lifting of a foot, except to stamp in indigation.

Armed with a set of directions and addresses, this fellow set out to establish telephonic contact with Pancho Gonzales, who tours the country playing professional tennis and registering financial discontent.

Director of the chase was Mr. Myron McNamara, who agents for Jack Kramer, who hires Gonzales (and others), who plays, he (Gonzales) insists, for peanuts.

"Now," said McNamara, "on Wednesday, between the hours of 2 and 3 P.M., Gonzales can be located at the Roger Smith Hotel in White Plains, New York. If not there, he can be located that night, between the hours of 7 and 8, at the County Auditorium in White Plains.

"If you should happen to miss him there, it'll be a cinch to find him at the Thomas Jefferson Inn in Charlottesville, Virginia, Thursday night. Should you miss him there, you might try at the University of Virginia where . . ."

. . . And then there is February, which has 28, except the years which it has 29. All the rest have 31, except those that have 30.

The desk clerk at the Roger Smith put forth valiant effort. "How do you spell it?" said he to the operator.

"S-m-i-t. . . ."

"No, no," said the clerk. "Mr. Pancho Whatshisname. How do you spell it?"

In a little while Mr. McNamara called back. He was jubilant. "He is at the Westchester Motor Court," he said. "He is driving his hot rod and he likes to stay out where he can tinker with it."

On the other end of the line Mr. McNamara could hear the sound of a headset hitting the floor.

It was a few hours later that Bryan M. Grant, formerly the "Giant-Killer," walked in.

"Driving his hot rod?" he said, and chortled. It isn't every day you hear a Giant-Killer chortle. "He may be a screwball, but he's the greatest—player, I mean."

The Giant-Killer sat still for a question, and you could see the hairs of his neck bristle.

"Now, how come you ask me something like that?" he said. "How can you compare Gonzales with Tilden? Everything has changed, style and everything. Gonzales has that powerful serve, then he charges the net. Tilden played an all-court game, and he was great.

"It's like trying to compare Bob Feller and Walter Johnson. Everything has changed."

The long distance operator called back and reported that Gonzales couldn't be located in Charlottesville. There was no room in the inn and Gonzales had gone to a motor court where he could tinker with his hot rod.

A little later Mr. McNamara walked in, harassed and annoyed. "Hot rod!" he snorted, as best he can snort. He is a soft man and not built for snorting. "He had his brother drive that fool thing all the way across the country for him. He'll kill himself in it yet."

Mr. McNamara, finally becalmed, sat down and soulfully considered the vocal tug of war between Gonzales, the star, and Kramer, the promoter.

"Of course I'm on Kramer's side, so I can only see it his way," he said. "Jack's lawyer tells him he has an ironclad contract with Gonzales. Gonzales' lawyer tells him he has a loophole and can get out.

"What Pancho seems to want to do is run his own tour. Well, I'd like for him to get a look at the books. When he sees what Jack makes and when he sees what he's making, he'll run back to his racket. Nobody but Kramer would take such a risk.

"Last year he paid Tony Trabert $118,000 and Gonzales $50,000. That's a big nut to crack, but Jack's willing to take the risk. There's no doubt about it, Pancho is the greatest. Nobody in the world can beat him. I'm still a Kramer man. I say Jack could have beat him in his prime, but maybe he couldn't.

"Pancho is all power. He'll sweep you off the court with that serve. He is the big name—nobody denies that. I don't know how long these tours can go on without other new names. The amateur tournaments are our farm system, like pro football and the colleges. Sooner or later we may get around to 'open' tournaments. I'm sure we will. But until we do, the tour is the thing. Pancho's trying to knock it in the head.

"He's always wanted to be a baseball player. If he had, we'd have had another Ted Williams on our hands."

Spit and all.

DAZZY VANCE RE-DISCOVERED

(March, 1955)

(New life had come to the wilderness near Homosassa Springs, Florida, where Dazzy Vance maintained his peaceful retreat. His name had suddenly been called to the public's attention again. He had been elected to the Baseball Hall of Fame.

I had visited with him in his modest little cottage in the wild woods before. I simply stopped off one afternoon on the way to spring training and told him I wanted to talk to him because he was Dazzy Vance.

Now we were engaged in a more serious enterprise. He and I were becoming co-authors. "I'd Hate to Be a Pitcher Nowadays," he'd said, and that's exactly the title the SATURDAY EVENING POST *used on the story.)*

HOMOSASSA SPRINGS, FLA.—There isn't a man anywhere happier than Dazzy Vance has been lately. Once, he sat in his cabin by the side of the road and the race of men sped by. Now, the race has slowed some. It turns into the dusty little road that winds through the woods to the house where he lives, and together Dazzy and his friends sit and talk of his new glory.

"Nobody," he'll say, "ever would have give that 31-year-old feller that came to spring training with Brooklyn in 1922 a chance of ever being in the Hall of Fame. Now, would they?"

The obvious answer is a good and hearty "No." But there's old Daz, a new initiate of the Hall of Fame. It is sort of a res-

urrection for him, one of the great fast-ball pitchers of all time.
He had been secreted in his patch of woods a mile north of this
little spot on State Highway 19, the main street of Florida's
West Coast, and recalled only on rare occasions. Usually, it was
when somebody was trying to come up with a story about old
Wilbert Robinson and the Trolley Dodgers, as the Bums once
were known.

Dazzy had been around when he finally got to Brooklyn on
the recommendation of Nap Rucker, then the Dodgers' Southern scout. Pittsburgh had tried him and let him go, as did the
Yankees. He joined the Dodgers a pitching retread, eventually
won 198 games, led the National League seven seasons in strike-
outs and drew the highest salary ($35,000) ever paid a pitcher
up to his time.

"Look at this picture," Dazzy said. "All of these years, sixty-
three of them, I'd gone without having to wear one of them
things, and here I am, in my first tuxedo."

He fished the photograph out of a corrugated box full of
clippings and programs. There, holding their plaques at a New
York banquet, were Vance, Joe DiMaggio and Gabby Hartnett,
three of the newest Hall of Fame residents. Dazzy was smiling
broadly in the picture, but not nearly as genuinely as in the
flesh.

"By George," he said, "we ought to celebrate this. How about
a poor man's highball? You know what that is—with a little
sweetening in it."

He shuffled off into the kitchen to stir up some "poor man's
highballs," with a little sweetening in it. Mrs. Vance wasn't
there. She was tending their little Indian tepee gift shop on the
highway. These were Dazzy's days.

Why, just two nights before, the seventy-five people of Homosassa Springs had gathered at Hinson's restaurant and given a
big dinner for him. The Tampa papers were full of it that morning. Monday night he was to be the guest of honor at Governor
Leroy Collins' annual baseball dinner for the spring training
delegates.

There just wasn't much that hadn't been happening to old Daz lately.

Soon, he simmered down to the matter of pitching. Somebody had said something about the new rule chiseling down the size of the catcher's box.

"Everybody's putting in new rules," he said, "and every time they do it they make it tougher on the pitcher. They got so many rules now, like this silly twenty-second thing, that a fellow can't keep his mind on pitching for trying to keep from breaking the law. Now, you know, if you throw close to a batter they stop the game and come out to warn you.

"I never threw at but two batters in my life, and then I never threw at them because of something they did. You remember Earl Smith, the catcher? He was a good friend of mine, but he was with Pittsburgh. Well, he'd been riding me all day and it just got the best of me. I said to myself, 'I'm gonna knock down the next guy that steps up there.' It just happened to be Kiki Cuyler, who never had said a word to me. I knocked him down, too.

"The other time, Robby (Wilbert Robinson) had taken to calling the pitches from the bench, and on one particular pitch I'd never have made but for him, Irish Meusel of the Giants hit a two-run homer off me. Now, Irish was a good ball player, but he never got a hit off me before. This just made me mad, because there was a good game messed up because Robby was mad with our catcher and calling the signals.

"The more I thought the madder I got. George Kelly was the next batter up, old 'High-Pockets.' I just wound up and knocked him down. And George and me were good friends, but I had to throw at somebody. I really wanted to throw at Robby.

"One time when I was pitching against Cincinnati, I turned Babe Pinelli's cap bill around with a pitch that got away from me. The same Babe that's the umpire. Well, when he got to first he kept yapping at me. Then he started for the mound and I started toward him. It didn't make any difference to me. I was ready for him. But just before he reached me, I said to him:

" 'Babe, why don't you use your head? You know damn well that I don't knock down anybody but a good hitter.' That broke up that fight before it ever started."

It also broke up a short Sunday afternoon siesta, after which the guests went back to join the race of man.

Some . . . at Large

THE CUB NOBODY BELIEVED

(April, 1959)

(*This is a view from another angle of the most famous college football game ever played, when Georgia Tech discouraged Cumberland University, 222–0, on October 7, 1916.*

This was a big day in the life of the young reporter who is the central figure of the story, until, as you will see, ugly fate intervened in the form of doubting authority.

George Howard was one of my closest friends, a district sales manager for the White Truck Company in Atlanta, Georgia. One of his many qualities was that he seldom ever brought up a topic of sports. He was more considerably concerned at breakfast about the affairs of Little Orphan Annie.

I had known him for many years when, a short time before his death, he confessed to this brief but historic brush with journalism.)

George P. Howard Jr. died the other day, and with him went not only one of the world's most gentle and lovable souls, but also one of the last of the few untold truths of the most famous college football game ever played, and the worst.

George was not a famous man himself, except to those who got to know him well. To them he was famous for his companionship, not for exploits or go-getting or climbing in spiked boots over the fallen frames of fellow men in a mad drive for what our race calls The Top. He was, more than anything else, a dear friend who viewed me sometimes with tolerance and sometimes with pity, but never with an emotion that wasn't sincere.

George Howard had an early brush with athletics. In undergraduate days at Georgia Tech he was a member of the tennis team. He also had an early brush with journalism, and it was his debut that is this story. It happened on October 7, 1916, when he was a freshman at Georgia Tech.

The Howard family was a family of some circumstances in Atlanta, and George, consequently, had connections through which he was able to line up a job as campus sports correspondent for the Atlanta *Journal*. His first assignment was to cover this football game, by foot, walking the sidelines reporting a telephone play-by-play account to a rewrite man on the *Journal* desk.

Freshman Howard began with a report on the weather (fair and hot) and the crowd (about 1,000). He reported, too, that Tech won the toss but chose to kick off, which seemed somewhat radical, for John Heisman was a man greedy about his offense.

"Preas kicks off to Carney," George P., the freshman reporter, began, "who is downed in his tracks. Gouger goes over tackle for three yards. McDonald makes no gain in the center of the line. McDonald punts and Preas runs back to the Cumberland 20.

"Strupper sweeps right end for a touchdown. Preas kicks the extra point. Tech 7, Cumberland 0.

"Spence kicks off and Gouger returns to the Cumberland 10. Murphy fumbles, Guill recovers for Tech and scores a touchdown. Preas kicks the extra point. Tech 14, Cumberland 0.

All of this action had consumed something like 90 seconds of playing time.

"Preas bucks the line for a touchdown . . . Strupper runs for a touchdown . . . Shaver returns a punt seventy yards for a touchdown . . . Strupper sweeps end for sixty yards and a touchdown . . ." and this went on until Georgia Tech had a lead of 63–0 at the end of the first quarter.

"Boy, what's going on out there?" the suspicious rewrite man asked George Howard, the freshman. "Are you sure you know what you're doing?"

"Yes, sir," George said, "I'm giving it to you the way it happens."

"But no football team scores every time it gets its hands on the ball," the rewrite man protested.

"Maybe not," George Howard said, "but Georgia Tech's doing it."

About the middle of the second quarter, George felt a yank at his sleeve. "Here, boy," said the yanker, "let me have that telephone."

The rewrite man had been ordered to the football field by the managing editor. George protested. "If you don't believe I've got it right," he said, "check with the scorekeeper."

In those days the scorer sat at a table on the sidelines and he was an official of some stature. The rewrite man checked the scorer. To his disgruntlement, he found Tech's score was approaching 100 points, whereupon he mumbled an apology to George Howard and caught a trolley back to the *Journal* office.

It was something less than a mere coincidence that the freshman reporter was breaking in one one of sporting history's most incredible events. Georgia Tech beat Cumberland, 222–0.

Football scouting reports in those days were almost unheard of. Transportation was limited. Films were something that starred Francis X. Bushman and Theda Bara, and I might be out of historical orbit there myself. At any rate, word of football team strength traveled slowly and nobody in Atlanta knew anything of Cumberland, a little school in Lebanon, Tennessee, which was about to play its first and last game of the season.

Cumberland had no organized team, but a group of campus entrepreneurs had drafted sixteen misfits who "couldn't run with the ball, couldn't block and couldn't tackle," as Morgan Blake reported the next day. Only the Tech coaches knew how terrible it might be, and had shortened the quarters to twelve minutes and had allowed Cumberland first possession.

"It was not a football game, but a burlesque," Morgan Blake wrote. "It was a very ludicrous and amusing pastime."

George P. Howard Jr. was there, a rookie in his debut on the beat. Somehow, he never seemed to have much of an appetite for journalism after that.

THE HAPPY WANDERER

(December, 1958)

(*This was written at a time when football coaches were breaking ten-year contracts like dishes in a restaurant. In almost every deal was a package including a television show, and from coast to coast coaches were appearing on the air in the sponsored name of everything from potato chips to buttermilk.*

I took devilish delight in composing this simulated confessional of a brassy campus-jumper, letting the chips—potato or otherwise—fall where they may.)

★ ★

I am a football coach. The name is Bursitis, Charlie Bursitis. I've been around in this business. In fact, I guarantee you I've had more ten-year contracts than any coach around these days. Not to mention a couple for a lifetime.

You know what Harry Mehre says about his lifetime contract at Georgia. Three years later they declared him legally dead.

Well, ole Harry wasn't as hep as these coaches you got today. I just declare the school legally dead and move on. I'm 37 years old now, just turned in November. And if I'd filled every ten-year contract I've had, I'd be 95 going on 96.

The only coach I ever heard of living that long is A. A. Stagg, and he never was one of those driving, aggressive fellers. Just coaching, coaching, coaching.

You know, I'll bet he never had a TV show in his life. Nowadays, a football coach ain't nothing if he ain't got a TV show. Keeps him before the public. Shows up his sharp side. I've got a lot of respect for old A. A., though. Choice guy.

I've been around in this business, I said. First, I'll give you a little rundown on myself. Played my football at Alabama Seminary. I was All-America two years hand running. Really, I don't guess you could say I earned it my second year. I ran a motor scooter into a brick wall before the first game, cracked my skull and didn't play a-tall that season.

Well, when it come picking time the Illustrated News Service picked me on their first team. They were a little short on ends that season, but to tell you the truth, I had looked mighty good in practice before I got hurt.

I turned down a pro contract for $10,000 a year. I wanted to coach. I like to be out there with the boys. There's nothing better than being out there with the boys, seeing 'em grow and develop and go out into life. It does something to you here.

(Note: Tap left side of chest.)

I got me a job coaching the backfield at Jones-Vanberbilt U. The money wasn't too good and I moved to Kentucky Barber College the next year. We'd a-had a helluva record that year, but just before we played our big game two of our best linemen were caught breaking into a drive-in and it just wrecked us.

I moved on the next year to the Florida School of Sanitation, and if I do say so myself, we cleaned up down there. We woulda gone to a bowl game but the lousy basketball coach had been caught buying a plane ticket home for a boy with a sick mother, and the NCAA got us. That's the way the tough breaks go in this life.

Then I got lucky. Jasper Fenimore dropped dead walking across the campus at Fordyce College and they hired me to replace him. It was my big move. I was a head coach at last.

Had a great season my very first year, but nobody would take us in any bowl game. You know how Fordyce is, just a little school without much pull in the bigtime.

Well, I knew I couldn't stay there too long. Not enough action to suit me. The next winter, two days after I'd signed a ten-year contract, I got a call from T. C. (Top Cash) Mugford, the big alum that runs things at Sevierville A&M. He said they just had to have me there and would I come.

It just seems that people of destiny belong together, so I told 'em at Fordyce I really wasn't happy there. They released me from my contract and I went to Sevierville.

I stayed there a long time. Then two years later I moved to Sinclair State, then to Elmer Gantry U., then to Virginia Tech, then to Amarillo College, then to Palmolive U. and then to Western Oklahoma Normal.

That's where I am now, Western Oklahoma Normal. It's a fine school and I'm awfully happy here. My wife and kids, they just love it. Great place to bring up young 'uns.

Got fine facilities. You can't beat the scholastic standards. Everybody says they've got the best embalming school in the country. Our old grads are the leading undertakers in the country. You'll find their work in the best cemeteries. The president is my friend. The athletic director is like a father to me.

But the other night, I'm sitting at home and the telephone rings. It's Titus Blush, the alum that runs things at Alabama Seminary, the old school. He says that No-Nose Strunk is through as head coach there. Got to go.

Well, I'd read something like that in the papers, but I don't pay no attention to newspaper rumors.

"You got to come back," Titus said. "We need you. We won't take no for a answer. The old alums demand you. You're the onliest one that can save us."

I thought it over a long time. It wasn't a matter of money. It was my old school calling. It was like I was being pulled back by the silver cord. I couldn't seem to say no. I got a lifetime contract at Western Oklahoma Normal, I said to myself. President my friend. Athletic director like a father to me. Got herds of cattle named for me all over the state. But the mother school was calling. What could I do but . . .

My mind was made up. "Okay, Titus," I said, "but there's one thing we got to agree on."

"What," Titus said. He was breathless. "Ten-year contract. Sure. Lifetime? Just come."

"No, no," I said. "Just one thing. Do I get a TV show?"

(Note from TV Editor: "You can tune in any Friday night now on channel 13 and see Charlie Bursitis in his new TV show, called 'Coach Charlie Says'").

INSIDE FOOTBALL

(November, 1958)

(*It was Thanksgiving Day. The mother of my three boys—since increased to a squad of four—had just been shipped home from the hospital, where she had been under repair. She was recuperating splendidly, and we had her with us, and we were together, and that was the important thing.*

It cut into our customary Thanksgiving Day activities, such as attending the traditional Georgia–Georgia Tech freshman football game. This, mind you, is no affair to be snorted at. It is the biggest freshman game in the world, an annual sellout at 44,000.

Well, we had our alternatives, and we sat around the cozy fireplace or in the bedroom, ran from radio to television, and in general enjoyed a diversified day. By the time the sun set, my eardrums and my eyeballs were so sore I hated radio and television both.

You perhaps will recognize some of the characters herein. Lindsey Nelson is the NBC sportscaster. Thad Horton, once a Southern sportscaster, is now an advertising executive in New York. Charlie Tate coached the freshman team at Georgia Tech. And Red Grange is Red Grange.)

It was a perfect day for the Great American Dial Twister. The wind was out of the kitchen, a gentle zephyr heavily scented with roasting turkey and other Thanksgiving Day goodies. There wasn't a cloud in the ceiling and the field was as fast as a living room rug.

The all-male student body, consisting of three, was in fine voice. Our only cheerleader, a dreamy blonde, was not in top form. She had run into a surgeon's knife, which was why we were all there and not in the stadium.

Television won the toss, for the Detroit Lions and the Green Bay Packers were playing for brunch. First, though, there was a sobering note. The telephone rang and it was Detroit calling.

Pete Waldmeier said that H. G. Salsinger had died. He was one of the great names in sports writing until the very end. He teethed on the days of Ty Cobb and the raw, hardy times when people took horse cars to the ball park and never thought to complain about parking conditions.

Salsinger had died at 8:45 and the people were trying to locate Cobb. Salsinger and Cobb had been great friends, and there are pictures in Ty's collection of the two out in the hunting fields.

Back on television, Detroit and Green Bay had already assumed a 7-7 position, but the Packers were backed up against their own wall. Max McGee, who didn't learn such shenanigans at Tulane, decided he'd run on a fourth-down punt situation from his 19-yard line. The snap wasn't good, but neither was the judgment, for Detroit threw him a yard short and Jim Martin eventually used this opportunity to kick a field goal.

There was now a temporary truce declared while we indulged in the Thanksgiving feast, and we were all very thankful for everything.

When we returned to Detroit and Green Bay, the Packers were cutting up and took the lead, 17-14. Then it started snowing in Detroit, and our all-male student body loved this. They left their little fingerprints all over the screen trying to catch the flakes as they fell. Then they wondered why we couldn't order some for Atlanta.

Well, pretty soon McGee opened another closet door, and Green Bay was in trouble again. I should point out here that the Packers had already dropped behind again, not because of McGee, but because they do not have a barbed-wire defense.

Detroit got an extra one for insurance, after McGee tried another fourth-down run that failed, and the Packers and the

Lions took their leave. We all cheered enthusiastically and turned swiftly to other fields.

They were succeeded on the radio by Thad Horton with the Georgia-Georgia Tech freshman game, and on television by Lindsey Nelson and Red Grange with the Texas-Texas A&M game. We were the only people in the block with stereofusion sound.

Texas and Tech both took a lead in the first quarter, but the freshmen had been far more imaginative. Charlie Tate showed the crowd that he knew how to make ends meet. The thrifty Tech coach sent in John Ferguson, an end, to throw to Terry Evans, an end, off an old-fashioned end-around and John hit Terry for the touchdown. That ended that contest in a hurry.

Meanwhile, back at the ranch, Texas was disassembling Texas A&M. Rene Ramirez and Bobby Gurwitz, the two fellows who beat Georgia opening night, were having it all to themselves.

Texas A&M was bulding impressive statistics, but scratching nothing but the turf. Red Grange explained how this was.

"It's Charlie Milstead's passing against Texas' ground game," he said. "Milstead is fifth in the nation in total offense. He's second in passing in the Southwest Conference to Humphrey of Baylor. He has thrown for fifty-six yards while Texas hasn't completed a pass. A&M have five first downs to Texas' three, but . . ."

He hadn't been reading *Sports Illustrated* lately. People don't talk about statistics any more, it says.

Georgia fumbled and Tech recovered at Grant Field, Thad Horton said.

Ramirez scored another touchdown in Austin, where it was raining. Our student body said they didn't care for rain.

"There's a play you don't see often," Grange said, "a wide end run. Ramirez started outside and headed for the corner as fast as he could . . ."

That made sense.

Lee Reid and Larry Lafkowitz were running like they'll help that fullback situation some at Tech. But the score was still 6-0.

Ramirez was . . . oops, hold it. Stan Gann threw a pass to Terry Evans and Tech led, 12-0.

Ramirez started . . . then the sponsor called time out. There just hadn't been enough advertising. "Texas are looping and slanting and belaying the frotchit with a frim-fram," Grange said. 'You can make this work only in Thursday games, however. It won't go on Saturdays at all because the osteophorus is out of tune with the stremus, and no coach . . ."

Ah, man, his was inside football at its insidest. He was really laying it on the line now. He was losing our all-male student body, though. They decided it'd be more fun to eat again.

DUSTER TWITCHELL'S SECRET

(August, 1955)

★ ★ ★ ★ ★ ★ ★

(This was a day when sports broke out in a rash of kissing-and-telling. Everybody had a secret, as is explained in the process. There was no reason Grover (Duster) Twitchell couldn't have a secret of his own.)

★ ★

The name is Twitchell, Grover Twitchell. I am a southpaw pitcher. Several years ago I acquired the monicker of The Duster, which is what I am known as in the trade. I've got a secret.

I've been out of sight for a spell, hurling for Salt Rapids in the Three-Eye League which isn't exactly 20-20, but which they pay you well under the table in. I had my fling in the majors as a bullpen artist for the Chicago Cubs when Snorter Mahoney was the manager. Naturally, I want to get back to the majors, for like I always tell these kids, there's only one place to play this game and that's at the top.

You can quote me on that.

Secrets seem to be awful popular these days. Preacher Roe's got a secret. He throws a spitter. Joe Page has got a secret. He throws a spitter, too.

I see where Ben Hogan, the golf player, has got a secret. He says it's the way he helt his clubs when he was about to hit the ball. I read it over and I swear I don't think that magazine got its money's worth of secret myself. That's the way I been holding my clubs for years and everybody's been saying it's a mistake.

I guess this is just the season for confession and every magazine's got to have somebody confessing something to be popular. But back to my secret.

Like I said, I had a stretch with the Chicago Cubs when Snorter Mahoney was manager. That's when it happened. The reason I'm not saving this for no magazine is that ever guy and his brother that ever pitched a baseball claims that he's the feller. But actual, I'm the guy. I done it myself. Listen close now.

I invented the slider.

In fact, I'm the only hurler in the country that throws a natural, genuine slider. In fact, it's the only thing I can throw, which is why I'm down here in Salt Rapids. Everybody knows that the next pitch is going to be a slider, so I can't fool them guys any higher any longer. The way bullpen artists goes these days, though, I keep thinking that some of these clubs might need me around for just one pitch or two. That's how I think I'll get back, and I'm not but 41, just a boy in the bud, which brings me back to my story.

When I am with the Cubs there is this door that opens from the bullpen out on the street. When the days got awful hot, and you know they don't have lights at Wrigley Field, and it didn't look like Mahoney would be needing any bullpen artists, one of us would sneak down the streets to a little bar and pick up a few bottles of Bud.

Once in a while we'd get surprised and have to go to the mound and Snorter never could figure out why his artist would come in from the bullpen so happy. Old Tigermilk Baldwin got so bad he couldn't pitch except in that condition, which will surprise you as the reason for his being waivered out after that big year he had. Last time I heard of Tigermilk he was pitching for a brewery team in Nashville.

One day it was my turn to go for the suds. I was just fixing to leave the bar with the bag in my arms. They had the radio tuned in on the game and I heard the announcer say that

Mahoney was looking towards his bullpen. Bull Egbert, who was our ace, had come down with a stomach ache and had to have an artist to help him.

"Naturally," the announcer said, "Mahoney'll want old Duster Twitchell to come in here and pitch to Stan Musial, him being the southpaw that he is."

I lit out up the street like a mad dog and I hammered on the door for them to let me in the bullpen. Nobody paid me no attention, and later I found out why. I stuck the big finger of my left hand through a knothole and that was my mistake. Something hit it like a mule stepped on it and I saw more stars than they are in Hollywood.

What happened was, old Snorter had come out to the bullpen hisself to see why I wasn't warming up. All the other artists was pitching like crazy and when he saw that finger come through the knothole he knew it was me. He whomped it with a empty beer bottle, which wasn't hard to find in our bullpen.

Well, he fined me $100, which I paid humble like, but my real trouble hadn't begun. This big knot rose on my finger and it wouldn't go down. First time I warmed up after that, Jinks Applegate, the catcher, hollered:

"Hey, what was that you throwed?"

I told him the thing sort of slid off that knot, and that's how it got the name. Jinx called it "that sliding thing." But the knot never went away. Everything I throwed was a slider. I went from Chicago to L. A. to Ponca City to Nashville to Spokane and all around to Salt Rapids and that slider went right along with me. And my knot went with me. I throw the beautifulest slider you ever saw but that's all.

I see where all these pitchers say the slider was the making of them. It just ruint me complete, and that's a true story as sure as my name is Duster Twitchell.

MANHATTAN ON THE ROCKS

(June, 1958)

(On a summer vacation in New York, I found to my dismay that the old island was exceedingly dull with the Giants and the Dodgers transferred to the West Coast. This was the first summer of their geographical transgression, and adjustment to the violent change had not yet taken place.

One evening I watched the Philadelphia–Pittsburgh game and another evening I watched the Philadelphia–St. Louis game, both piped into this metropolitan retreat. The late shows were of late vintage, however.

It really wasn't too much of a strain for a tourist. It released me for indulgence in other channels, such as the harness races at Roosevelt Raceway and engrossing musical sessions at the Embers.)

NEW YORK—This is a ghost town. You walk into Toots Shor's and where you used to see the old baseball line gathered in, now you see their ghosts, or unemployed actors, or television performers going on or coming off duty, and in either case, seeking liquid fortification.

You go to Madison Square Garden and it's dead. Everywhere you see unhabeased corpuses laid out, from Cesar Brion to Rocco Marchegiano. The cauliflower shop is closed. Except that on Friday, Saturday and Sunday you could have seen the Moiseyev Russian Dance Company, but this would have got you to sniffling about Joey Maxim, a nifty ballet man.

You will find action at Ebbets Field. The specters are still active there, roaming the empty stands, wailing and bawling, ringing cowbells and shouting for De Dook to nail some bum for another four-ply swat, or for Oiskin to strike out some bum, or for some bum to do something.

The bodies are still warm here, for the Dodgers have just recently departed this sacred pasture. From the air, Ebbets Field still looks like the same old asylum, but it also looks depressingly vacant. They promise that there will be "lively activity, a series of unusual first appearances in New York of sports and feature events."

But first blood has yet to be drawn.

The Polo Grounds is somewhat better organized. There was no doubt that the Giants were gone and the ghosts were able to take possession immediately after Dusty Rhodes broke his bat grounding to short for the last out last September. And so you could run up to Harlem and see a rodeo fertilizing the Shrine of St. Wilfred Mays.

No less than Al Tansor's World Championship Rodeo. And all who have ever heard of Al Tansor will please stand and be counted.

Even Yankee Stadium has been taken over by strange spirits. The Indianapolis Clowns and three other Negro teams were playing there. Any resemblance between them and their landlord ended with the line on the ticket identifying the site of conflict.

This was the baseball attraction. New York has been two or three weeks without major league baseball. Oh, there was greater selectivity for the stay-at-home, though.

He had his choice of the Phillies, with entrancing suggestions on choice of vermouth and wine; the Pirates, delivered direct to the parlor by a beer producer; or the Yankees, piped back home by still another beer and ale dispenser.

"Never," said an old journalism acquaintance, "have our kids had such latitude in selecting their form of delinquent diversion. You think the old New York was rough-hewn. Now the young chap has his choice. He can go to hell in a handy six-pak, or with a glass of iced sherry. Urgh!"

You got to say this for it. It's the best-covered ghost town since Sleepy Hollow, which may have been just a location and not incorporated. The sporting authors are bobbing up in the least-expected places looking for a new twist.

At Roosevelt Raceway the other evening there were three of the city's busiest columnists. Usually this is a season's quota for the harness racing campus on Long Island, which usually goes about its wealthy way and medicates its slight with greenback grease. Now it finds itself a very popular retreat for journalists.

"Then there are evenings of sitting at home taking your pick of the three television games, and beer, vermouth or wine," James J. Cannon of the *Post*, said, "and suddenly you snap out of it like a guy with the laughing gas turned off. You look around to see if anybody has been staring at you.

"Then you catch the first train out of town and go looking for some place where there is something happening."

It doesn't have to be Big. Last weekend Cannon went to Cincinnati to see the Redlegs play Los Angeles.

The other day they held a football coaching clinic about ninety miles up the country from this lonely isle. Columnists and other authors swarmed the place. Used to be, a coaching clinic stirred up the tribe in Manhattan like a taffy pull. A new harness racing plant opens up in the Catskills, too, and there already has been much buzzing about this.

The horses race on. You catch a train to Belmont, a boat to Monmouth, a bus to Roosevelt, drive up to Yonkers or fan out on greater adventures to Narragansett or Delaware Park. This is not to say horse racing is not dead, but that gambling quite definitely is much alive.

But there was encouragement on the way in from the airport. Just outside LaGuardia Field a whole slue (a great number) of kids had a baseball game going on a vacant lot. A few blocks away some older men, apparently just off the day shift, were seriously engaged in a playground game. Then, of all things, on a concrete area no larger than left field in Los Angeles, a bunch of fellows had a pickup game going on a side street.

Obviously there is still some sentiment for baseball up here. No one has really yet determined whether it's for or against. The town's too near dead to get a pulse.

A HARD WEEK ON CELEBRITIES

(March, 1959)

(*It is right much of a challenge to make a field trial sound as exciting as it really is. Exhilarating, I should say.*

There's something about arising at 5:30 in the morning, breakfasting at 6 and climbing in a saddle to ride eight hours on a chilly day that hardly encourages the use of the word exciting. It is an exhilarating experience, though, beginning with the ride through the dawn over sandy rural lanes to the starting point. At first contact, the feel of the saddle is a little rude, but this wears off in awhile.

Get a good working horse and it can be a day of pleasure. Get an ornery one and it can be a day you should have spent in bed.

The field trial circuit hits the Southeast from January to March. You can't stay too long, or else each column begins to read like the last one. But for a day or two, it's wonderful sport.

This was a most rewarding field trial excursion, first because there were some celebrated dogs at the Continental, and second because I had a good horse.)

★ ★

QUITMAN, GA.—The brambles, defiant and prickly, were green with tender new leaves encouraged by a false spring. Pretty buds had popped out on the wild plum and cherry trees, dabbing a dash of nature's own colors in the hedgerows. The dead cornstalks, standing in decadent disarray, were evidence enough that winter had visited here, though.

The frigid season was not totally spent. The nip in the air and the brazen wind that burned exposed cheeks told you this.

And then the sky was heavy with sullen clouds that had the threat of snow in them.

"The wind's from the east," Bill Allen had said, "and that's bad. I don't know why, but a dog just can't find any birds with an east wind."

The Atlanta *Journal's* expert on such matters had proved his expertism again. Unfortunately, he himself had to be the victim, he and Herb Holmes of Springfield, Illinois. They had put their dogs down at 8:15 Saturday morning, Herb's Gunsmoke and Bill's Commander's Hightone Rambler, who is addressed as Nip, and that was the last that had been seen of them. After twenty minutes they were declared out of judgment, and the people were now riding gallery on a fresh brace.

It was tragic enough for Bill, who was taking the setback hard, but it was a fate even more unjust for old Gunsmoke. He was the defending champion in the National Amateur Quail Championship, won it last year at Carbondale, Illinois. Eventually both he and Nip showed up back at the kennel, but they had been dealt out.

The old white horse flailed through the mucky underfooting of the field, ignoring the dead cornstalks, and pushed on over the ridge. Carl Duffield, a warmhearted Texan, was working Lady Commander Zev and a point had been called. The handsome setter had her nose aimed at a patch of undergrowth. Somewhere back over the ridge you could hear George Suttle hallooing for Cross Smoke, his pointer and the other half of the brace.

Carl dismounted, lashed through the undergrowth in honor of Lady's point, but there were no birds.

"That east wind," Bill muttered, "that cussed east wind. It even crossed up the champion."

Gunsmoke was in high-class company as an unseated champion. It had, in fact, been a hard week on celebrities.

Wednesday afternoon, Palomonium had made his appearance here, fresh from his second glorious national bird dog championship at Grand Junction, Tennessee. This is the World Series, this week at Grand Junction.

Palomonium was braced with another pointer, Northwester, the property of Guy Lewis of Orange, Virginia, president of the American Field Trial Association. It was a match in which the grand champion had come off second best. Northwester had scored four clean finds. Palomonium had scored three finds, one of which was questionable, and one unproductive.

The National Amateur gets its name from the trainers' status, not the dogs'. An owner coming to this event handles his own dog. This is the sportsman's game. Only amateur handlers, those who do not hire out as trainers, can handle dogs in this championship.

This explains the appearance of Palomonium, most definitely not an amateur at quail discovery. His owner, Jimmy Hinton, a Tuscaloosa (Ala.) dairyman, handled him here. Palomonium usually is handled by Clyde Morton of Union Springs, Alabama, one of the great names in the trade.

Clyde produced the championship at Grand Junction. Then there was the switch to his owner, Hinton, here. This makes it sound as if Hinton takes the blame for Palomonium's performance.

"There is," Carl Duffield said, "a lot of luck in this game. First, you've got to have birds. Then it doesn't make a lot of difference who's handling a dog like Palomonium. He's the kind of dog that handles his handler."

There was now another brace to be set down, Wildfair Riley, owned by John Grant, and Q's Delivery Doone, owned by Harold Crane. They worked their way back toward the lunching place, a little white building trimmed in green somewhere over the rolling 36,000 acres of Mrs. Gerald M. Livingston.

This, it should be said, is one of the remaining strongholds of old Southern plantation living, though Mrs. Livingston, the gracious queen of the little empire—it is considerably larger than Grace Kelly's Monaco—is from New Jersey.

Dixie Plantation is dedicated to the improvement of the breed of bird dogs and walking horses, to the proposition that there will always be birds, and that gracious guests will enjoy gracious hospitality in the antebellum magnificence of the red brick mansion that poses a striking picture through the stone gates.

The plantation sits about ten miles south of Quitman and sprawls over the state line into Florida. We had ridden over both states following the courses of the morning.

Riley and Delivery Doone had been picked up and the horses began gathering at the lunching place. The two judges, Ike Brandon and W. J. Heisler, put their heads together. Palomonium was there. Jimmy Hinton had driven in from Tuscaloosa with his liver-spotted champion for the decision.

Brandon and Heisler came out of session. They had reached a decision. The new national amateur quail champion was Northwester. Runner-up was Newman's Delivery Dan, owned by E. J. Newman. Also ran: Palomonium.

Palomonium didn't charge from the dugout and protest to the umpire. He didn't parade around the ring with his forepaws clutched in self-appointment to victory. He didn't stand up and scream at the referee. He took it like a . . . well, like a champion.

He just stood there licking his chops. Jimmy Hinton took it like a champion, too. He led Palomonium back to his car and they drove down the sandy road on their way back to Union Springs.

THE 'ANGEL,' THE DEVIL AND THE CHAMPION

(March, 1961)

(*This was the report of a tour around Miami the day before Floyd Patterson made it two out of three over Ingemar Johansson in the prize fight ring.*

I visited Bill McDonald on his yacht that morning at Bal Harbour. I dropped in on fight headquarters and Billy Graham's adjacent revival meeting shortly after lunch. And I finished up with a late afternoon call on Patterson at his rented stucco headquarters on Pinetree Dr.

It will be observed that the contrast fascinated me—millionaire sportsman, evangelist and old-time religion, fight mob, and then the homey atmosphere of the kitchen in the home where the champion lived. It was a rewarding day.)

★ ★

MIAMI BEACH—Floyd Patterson and Ingemar Johansson would fight for the heavyweight boxing championship of the world Monday at 10:30 P.M. in Miami Beach Convention Hall, and this was the man who had brought it off. His name is Bill MacDonald. He is round-faced, portly and with a matching disposition. You know, all the world loves a fat man.

He stood on the deck of his yacht at Bal Harbour on a bright Sunday morning. The breeze was gentle. The harbor water lapped lazily at the hull of "Snoozie."

Men of the fight game and newspapering were gathered on the fantail. MacDonald stood among them wearing his navy blue commodore's coat and cap.

He is rich and a sportsman. He made $7,000,000 manufacturing mobile homes. He said so himself. He once was the doorman at the Dempsey-Vanderbilt.

"I bought 'the door' for $750 and made $8,800 in one season," he said.

He finances golf tournaments for the PGA, owns race horses, owns 45 per cent of Tropical Park race course and three minor league baseball clubs. Then a man named Dave Feld came to him and told him he thought he could get Patterson-Johansson for Miami Beach. MacDonald would have to help.

"I met Cus D'Amato at the World Series and we talked," MacDonald said. "They were talking about a $600,000 guarantee at the gate. I said $400,000. D'Amato said the fight was going where he said, because he was Patterson's manager.

"When he came down to $400,000, it was a deal. In other words, I underwrote the fight for Miami Beach. D'Amato later told me that after he talked to me, he knew the fight was going to go only one place—Miami Beach.

"I looked into it good first. I didn't want to get in a racket with hoodlums and crooks, and you know how boxing is known. I liked D'Amato. He's an odd guy, but I think he's honest. That sold me, his honesty.

"A fellow's trying to get me to buy Sonny Liston's contract now. I don't know. He's a good boy, but I just want to make sure if I buy him I don't buy a lot of guys in the back room, too."

In Convention Hall Sunday afternoon, Billy Graham was preaching. Where 14,000 fight fans would sit and shriek for blood and slaughter eighteen hours later, 14,000 people had come in out of the tropical sun to listen to this magnetic man.

You could hear the voices singing even as you parked your car. It was an old-time hymn we used to sing in the little white clapboard church on a Sunday morning back home in North Carolina.

In the lobby of Convention Hall, members of the fight mob,

going to and from the press room, would stop and talk in hur-
ried tones, then rush on.

"Christ-a-mighty," Mumbling Sam Sobel said, waving a burning cigar dangerously near the nose of a listener, "this so-and-so
thinks he can push me around, and I . . ."

George Beverly Shea sang "All Hail the Power of Jesus'
Name" in the background.

"Damn, what a helluva mob that guy's drawed in there," said
an intellectual. "You see de money dey just carried out?"

Billy Graham's powerful voice poured through the public
address system now. The worshippers had opened their Bibles
and were reading the text for the day's sermon. Behind
and above Graham's head a huge blue and white banner
read:

"Jesus says, 'I am the way, the truth and the life.'"

The 14,000 sat now and listened intently, and you stood and
thought of the incongruousness of it all. Here, one man battled
the devil man-to-man, fought, strove, beseeched souls to save
themselves. Over 900 persons had marched down the aisles the
night before and joined him.

On the next evening, the place would be turned over to the
slaughterers, the morbid whose idea of gay entertainment is the
sight of a left jab stinging the cheek, a hard right to the skull or
the sight of a referee in white, vigorously counting out the benediction over the fallen body of some poor pug—they would pay
up to $100 for seating space.

Outside in the hallways, the fight mob milled about and
cursed on. They still wondered how much money the ushers
had toted out that afternoon.

In the kitchen of the white stucco house at 2815 Pine Tree
Drive, Floyd Patterson was getting a haircut. He stuck his hand
out from under the barber's apron. He said he felt fine. He said
this was no ritual. He said he was just getting his every-two-
weeks haircut.

"I understand that some people won't get their hair cut before
a match or a game because it is supposed to be weakening," the

heavyweight champion of the world said. "Do you think there's anything to that?"

"It comes from the story of Samson, I guess," somebody said. "A lot of baseball pitchers don't shave before a game."

"Oh, I don't shave, either," Patterson said. "There's something about the beard that toughens your skin, I think."

A photographer crept in from the living room and began snapping pictures of him from all angles with a camera shaped like a stick of bologna. Patterson paid no attention.

In the dining room just outside, Cus D'Amato shifted restively in his seat. "Too many people coming in this place," he muttered. "It ought to be quiet around here today."

This is a residential home in a quiet, middle bracket residential section. Patterson and his party rented it for a month. It cost him $2,300, without downstairs furniture. Everything but a few chairs and a dining table was moved out.

"I'll have a steak tonight and I'll go to bed at 10 o'clock and get up at 10 o'clock tomorrow morning," Patterson was saying in the kitchen.

He said he'd sleep most of that time. "I haven't dreamed much this time. Last time I kept dreaming that Johansson's right was on the way to my chin, but I always woke up before it hit. I haven't dreamed about it this time."

When someone mentioned Sonny Liston to him, Patterson said carefully, "If I beat Johansson, I think that Sonny Liston is the next man to fight."

Friday evening he had gone to Convention Hall. "Billy Graham wanted to meet me," he said. Patterson is a Catholic, a convert.

"We are giving up the hall Monday night only," Graham had told the audience. "Every other night I will preach here. On Monday night, Floyd Patterson will preach."

Patterson enjoyed telling the story. He grinned pleasantly. He said good-by. Outside, Sunday was bright and sparkling. Outside 2815 looked just like any other house on Pine Tree Drive.

A FAREWELL TO WALLACE

(For weeks it had been known within a tight little circle of insiders that Wallace Butts would resign as football coach at the University of Georgia. Announcement was being withheld until after the bowl season, and so I started my Christmas vacation without any fear of losing the story.

One morning in a large department store in Atlanta, a Christmas shopping trip with my wife was interrupted by a page over the public address system. The story had leaked out. Butts' resignation was public knowledge.

My vacation came to a sudden end, and I rushed to my trusty Royal to compose this laudation in behalf of a little chubby-faced fellow who had been a football coach in spite of a severe shortage of physical qualifications, who could be happier, who could be sadder, and who had more pride than a penful of peacocks.)

This was the irony of it, classic irony. On the day that Wallace Butts' resignation as head football coach at Georgia leaked out, he was being matriculated in the Helms Foundation Hall of Fame.

As they say about a victim of a heart attack who has just departed this earth without prior notice, that's the way to go. In the case of Butts, the announcement from Helms headquarters in Los Angeles was emphatic testimony to his stature in the trade which he has chosen to leave.

Butts' decision is accepted with regret by all of those who know him for the plump, complex package of humanity which he is. To assume that he is ready to put himself out to pasture is ridiculous. I am sure that his competitive spirit will not be watered down even one dram by the administrative office to which he has remanded himself, a position which ordinarily indicates the deteriorating advance of age.

If I may border on pure desecration of a sacred ceremony, I feel that the day they haul his remains out into the cemetery they'll have to hold him down to close the lid on the box.

If I should say that the news of Butts' resignation as an active coach came as news to me, I would be guilty of a bald-faced lie. Knowledge of his intended decision reached me the third week in November. I discussed it with him then and several times since.

Except for the brief period of exhilaration following his fourth straight victory over Georgia Tech, he hasn't wavered. Once again, as they say, this is the way to go.

Leave 'em laughing. Leave 'em happy. Leave 'em remembering you as a winner over Georgia Tech in four straight years, the winner of a bowl game, and a man shouldered and given free transportation out of Sanford Stadium on the occasion of his last appearance.

And so after 21 years, 11 months, 23 days, and about two hours, James Wallace Butts has had his day as the head coach of football at Georgia.

The beginning was recorded in a story in the Atlanta *Journal* on December 31, 1938. The actual act of confirmation took place the next day, January 1, 1939.

The end, by coincidence, also took place in the Atlanta *Journal* of December 23, 1960. At that time, Coach Butts and his wife, Winnie, were in transit to Montgomery, Alabama, where next week he concludes his coaching career in the Blue-Gray game.

I say that, but I'm not altogether sure that the conclusion is the sort of thing that can be considered positive, definite or irrevocable. A year or two in the confinement of administration, of piloting a desk in an office removed from the fast traffic of activity may bring out Butts screaming for a challenge.

He is, however, staunch in his position at the moment.

"This'll probably add ten years to my life," Wally told me the other day, "and if it doesn't, it'll add ten years to Winnie's life. It's almost as tough on a wife as it is on a coach.

"This has been a hard row to hoe with the recruiting problems we've had at Georgia. Some people appreciate what you do and some don't, but that's not important to me. The most important thing to me is the University of Georgia, and it always has been, and that's why I'm doing it now."

There was one other thing to be said. No coach ever gave Georgia such prosperity. No Georgia coach ever collected such an impressive lot of honors for the school and for himself. No coach ever worked harder, stayed up later, got up earlier and battled more violently for Georgia.

"I've thought it over," Wally said. "I've had every honor that a coach can get, except the coach of the year nationally. I've won 225 games coaching in high school and college, and that would take about 25 years of winning 10 a year, and that's a pretty good record.

"I'm not going to go away embarrassed, anyway. I've tried to give Georgia everything I had and I think that most people appreciate it. I've been loyal to Georgia ever since I came here and I always will be."

There were times in the depths of the depression in which Georgia wallowed during the mid-'50s that for the good of the school and for himself his departure would have been an act of discretion. The school was split within itself, some devoted to Coach Butts and some to the honor of the university.

Still, he clung to his position with doggedness. If he went, he'd go only on the toe of somebody's boot. He wouldn't move voluntarily. Fortunately, there were enough ever-faithful devotees behind him never to allow the anti-Butts faction to undermine him. His resurgent record is bold evidence that his cunning as a coach never wavered.

Just what Georgia will be like without Wallace Butts as head coach is a scene difficult to picture. Like Niagara without the falls, like Amos without Andy, like Coca-Cola in square bottles. He ran the emotional gamut from tantrums to baby sweetness, but never, never did he run from a fight.

He was widely known for his tearful approach to the game of the morrow. Yet, I don't think he ever really expected to lose until the ultimate outcome became unqualifiedly apparent.

Somehow, from somewhere there would come supreme intervention in his behalf and it all would work out for the Bulldogs and the best. Somehow, I'm sure he feels that so will this.

TY COBB . . . THE MOTIVATING FORCE

(July, 1961)

(Ty Cobb had come home to Georgia about three years before. He had bought a plot of land on top of a mountain near Cornelia, where he planned to build his first house after seventy-one years of roaming.

Actually, he had come home to die. He wanted to settle here, but every time he got close to building, something stopped him. Loneliness and the vast gap between his boyhood in this region and the present made him feel uncertain. Everything he did and said spoke of this doubt, but he talked firmly of his plan.

I spent several harrowing days wallowing in the torpor of his uncertainty, trying to construct "A Visit With Ty Cobb" for the SATURDAY EVENING POST. *The story finally was written, but Ty never was quite certain that it was the thing to do.*

My family and I had just arrived at Hilton Head, a lovely coastal retreat off South Carolina's "Low Country" mainland, for a vacation when the news arrived that Cobb had died of cancer. This column had to be constructed in a hurry. About the house, it never was built.)

★ ★

HILTON HEAD, S. C.—The news that Ty Cobb had died reached Hilton Head early Monday afternoon, and by sundown it was the most reverently discussed topic among the clientele of the William Hilton Inn, gathered in clots by poolside, in the little red-leather lounge and in the dining room. He had not struck a home run, or stolen a base, or filed a spike in thirty-three years. But this was the kind of hold the man had on the public.

The news of death came as no shock. It had been expected for several days. Yet, the realization that the Georgia Peach was no longer among the living created a strange emptiness.

Whatever one feels for such a man as Cobb, be it respect, awe, or idolatry, it is tempered at such moments by the realization that there is no immortality. Only the records exist now to preserve the name in a perspective that will vary with the erosive effects of the years that will come to pass.

Remembrances are aroused. You see him in many settings and in many moods, at the table of his dining room in California, at home plate in Ponce de Leon Park, in a hotel room in New York City, but most vivid of them all is the memory of him in the living room in the antebellum home in Cornelia, Georgia.

He had come back to Georgia to build a home on the top of Chenocetah Mountain. He was drifting about in obvious uncertainty. A sentimental plot was imbedded in his mind, but impeded by an unwillingness to shut himself off in self-appointed isolation.

"I'm tired," he said, sinking into an easy chair in the home he had rented while he contemplated his plans.

"I'm old and I'm tired. I don't like to say I'm old, but I am. It has been a tough life, twenty-four years of fighting off Lajoie, Jackson, Collins, Speaker and Ruth. Trying to stay ahead of them. I had to do that era after era."

This was the utterance that smote you. I remember I sat up straight with surprise. This was a moment that I marked in my life as rich history.

He talked on. I didn't dare breathe heavily, fearing I'd damage the entranced declaration of a great man's inner thoughts.

"I've used myself up since I was 17. I don't believe any player had a tougher time of it in baseball than I did. Now I'm 71 and tired and I want to get out of circulation. I'm going to be hard to find on my mountain."

From the top of the mountain the next day he pointed to a

house that sat small and plain in the valley. About where the settlement of Narrows used to be.

"Down there," he said, "in that little valley is the house where I was born. Not that one, but one close by. No one lives in it now, but it's still standing."

The smoke curled up from the chimney of the house in view and flattened out over the valley. You could imagine the baby child in the arms of his mother, remembered in those parts as a raven-haired beauty, and you looked at this soul-weary man beside you searching for something out of reach. A baby had gone out from that wilderness to the greatest fame an athlete could know, and you wondered what it could possibly be that he still sought.

It must have been something to fight for again. When he was on his mountain, there was nothing left but to sit and look down on his Georgia. This was rewarding in sentimental value but low in the measurement of self-achievement.

When he went away, he enjoyed notoriety, but when he went away he wanted to be back. He was fighting this battle to the death. There would never have been a truce.

It is for others to write of his battles on the field as a Detroit Tiger and Philadelphia Athletics player. Some of the motivating forces fascinate me more in the study of Cobb the aggressor.

All such men as this are complex. They never merely resort to emotion. They employ it until it soon overwhelms them. Cobb could be deeply sentimental. "I can cry," he once told me. "It runs in my family."

He could be vindictive, patronizing, arrogant, soft, violent, dramatic; but his emotional range never included apathy. What he felt at the moment, he felt with a passion that set him afire.

As he grew older, he grew more dedicated to the memory of his father, an educator and legislator from Royston. "My father was a man devoted to education," he said. "He was a school teacher, and a superintendent of county schools, then a state senator. He wanted to get me in position to get an appointment to Annapolis, but I had my mind set on baseball. My mind was made up.

"My father's devotion to education, that was the spark. That and the fact that I never went to college."

This is how he explained his establishment of the Cobb Educational Foundation for worthy but financially unqualified young men and women of Georgia.

He sat in the front porch swing of the Cobb home until 3 o'clock in the morning, arguing his case for baseball against his father's case for education, in the day of his youth. Finally, his father gave in. The next day, young Ty left for Augusta.

Another front porch scene took place in Royston many months later. Ty was on his way to Detroit now, called to the major leagues. His father lay a corpse in the funeral home. Ty listened to the story of how he had died, shot to death by his mother. Fire burned in his eyes and the words he spoke were inflammable. He would go out and get even with the world for this cruel stroke.

This was the activator. This drove him to play his fierce game. The ability was God-given. This was the force behind it.